HOLLOW

By Luke Cooper

Who is she?

She's a vigilante,
and she's a medium who allows
herself to be used as a vessel
for the vengeful dead.

The mask she wears represents
the face of the spirit within,
hiding her humanity as
well as her identity.

Her name is not important.
Her face is not important.
Her past is not important.

She is no one.

She is HOLLOW GIRL.

Creator, Writer and Artist: **Luke Cooper**

FOR **MARKOSIA ENTERPRISES** LTD

HARRY MARKOS
Publisher &
Managing Partner

GM JORDAN
Special Projects
Co-Ordinator

ANDY BRIGGS
Creative Consultant

IAN SHARMAN
Editor In Chief

Published by Markosia Enterprises, PO BOX 3477, Barnet, Hertfordshire, EN5 9HN. FIRST PRINTING, April 2023. Harry Markos, Director.

ISBN 978-1-915860-15-6

www.markosia.com

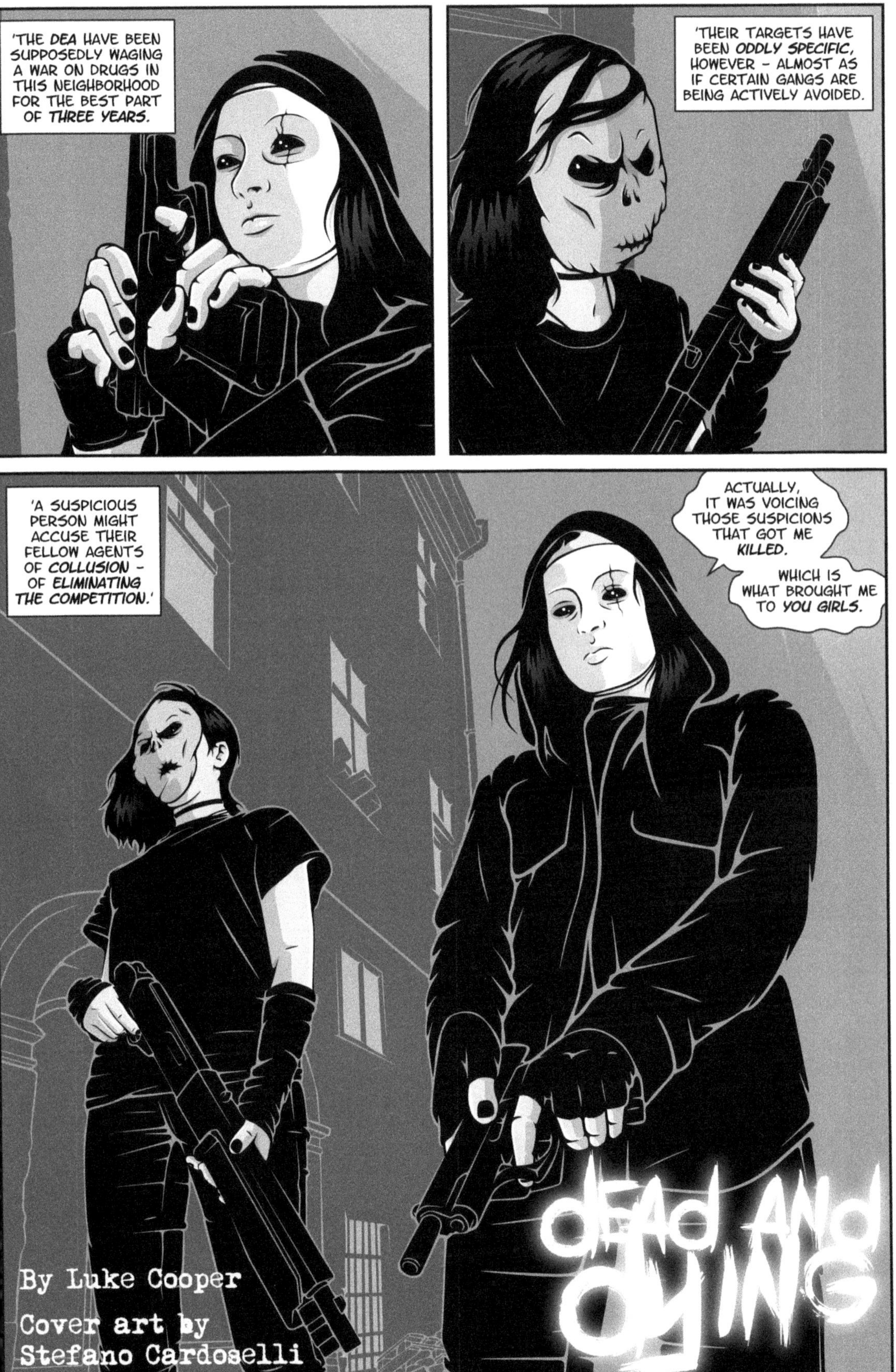
'THE DEA HAVE BEEN SUPPOSEDLY WAGING A WAR ON DRUGS IN THIS NEIGHBORHOOD FOR THE BEST PART OF THREE YEARS.
'THEIR TARGETS HAVE BEEN ODDLY SPECIFIC, HOWEVER - ALMOST AS IF CERTAIN GANGS ARE BEING ACTIVELY AVOIDED.
'A SUSPICIOUS PERSON MIGHT ACCUSE THEIR FELLOW AGENTS OF COLLUSION - OF ELIMINATING THE COMPETITION.'
ACTUALLY, IT WAS VOICING THOSE SUSPICIONS THAT GOT ME KILLED.
WHICH IS WHAT BROUGHT ME TO YOU GIRLS.
DEAD AND DYING
By Luke Cooper
Cover art by Stefano Cardoselli

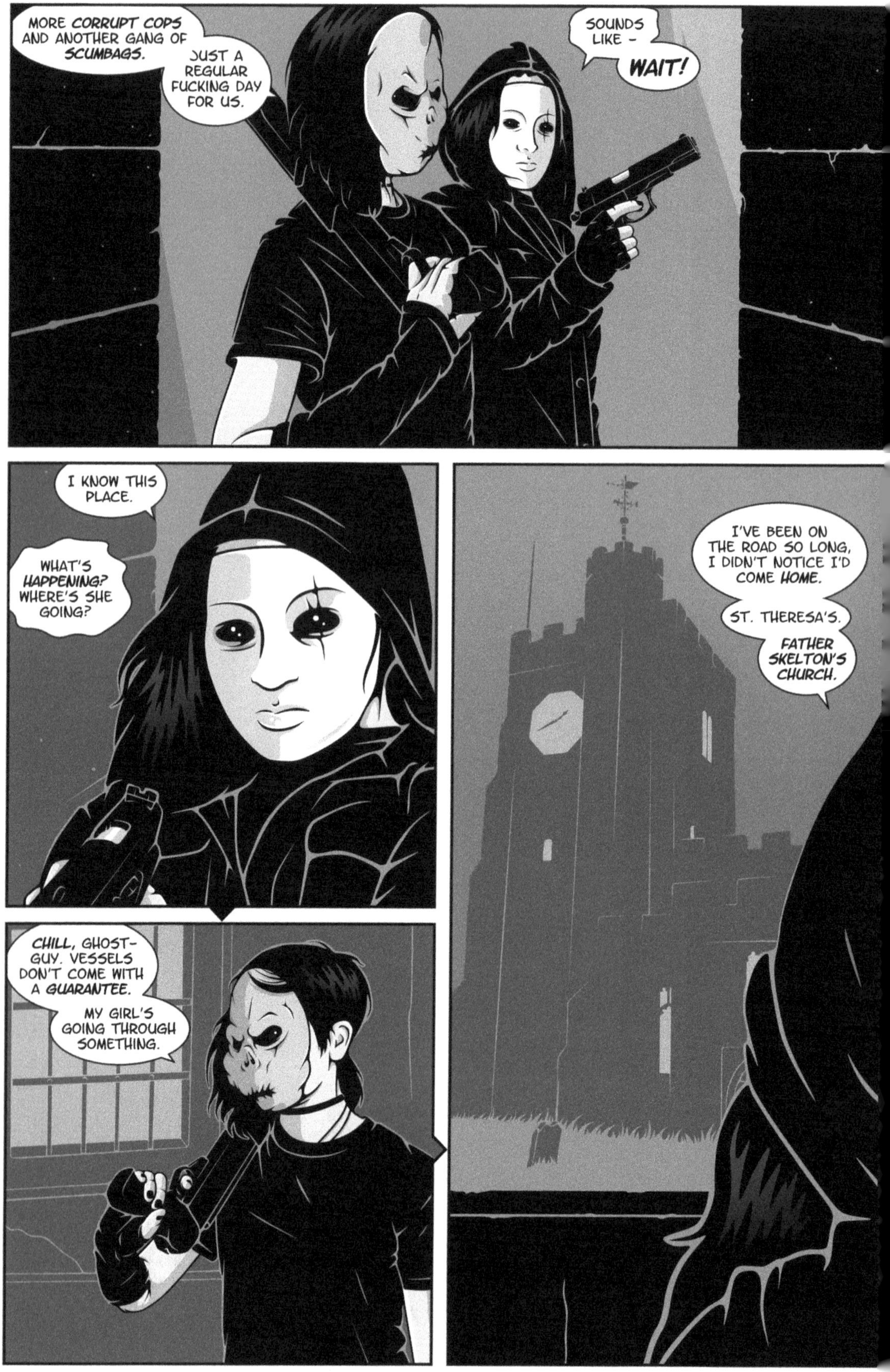
MORE CORRUPT COPS AND ANOTHER GANG OF SCUMBAGS.
JUST A REGULAR FUCKING DAY FOR US.
SOUNDS LIKE -
WAIT!
I KNOW THIS PLACE.
WHAT'S HAPPENING? WHERE'S SHE GOING?
CHILL, GHOST-GUY. VESSELS DON'T COME WITH A GUARANTEE.
MY GIRL'S GOING THROUGH SOMETHING.
I'VE BEEN ON THE ROAD SO LONG, I DIDN'T NOTICE I'D COME HOME.
ST. THERESA'S.
FATHER SKELTON'S CHURCH.

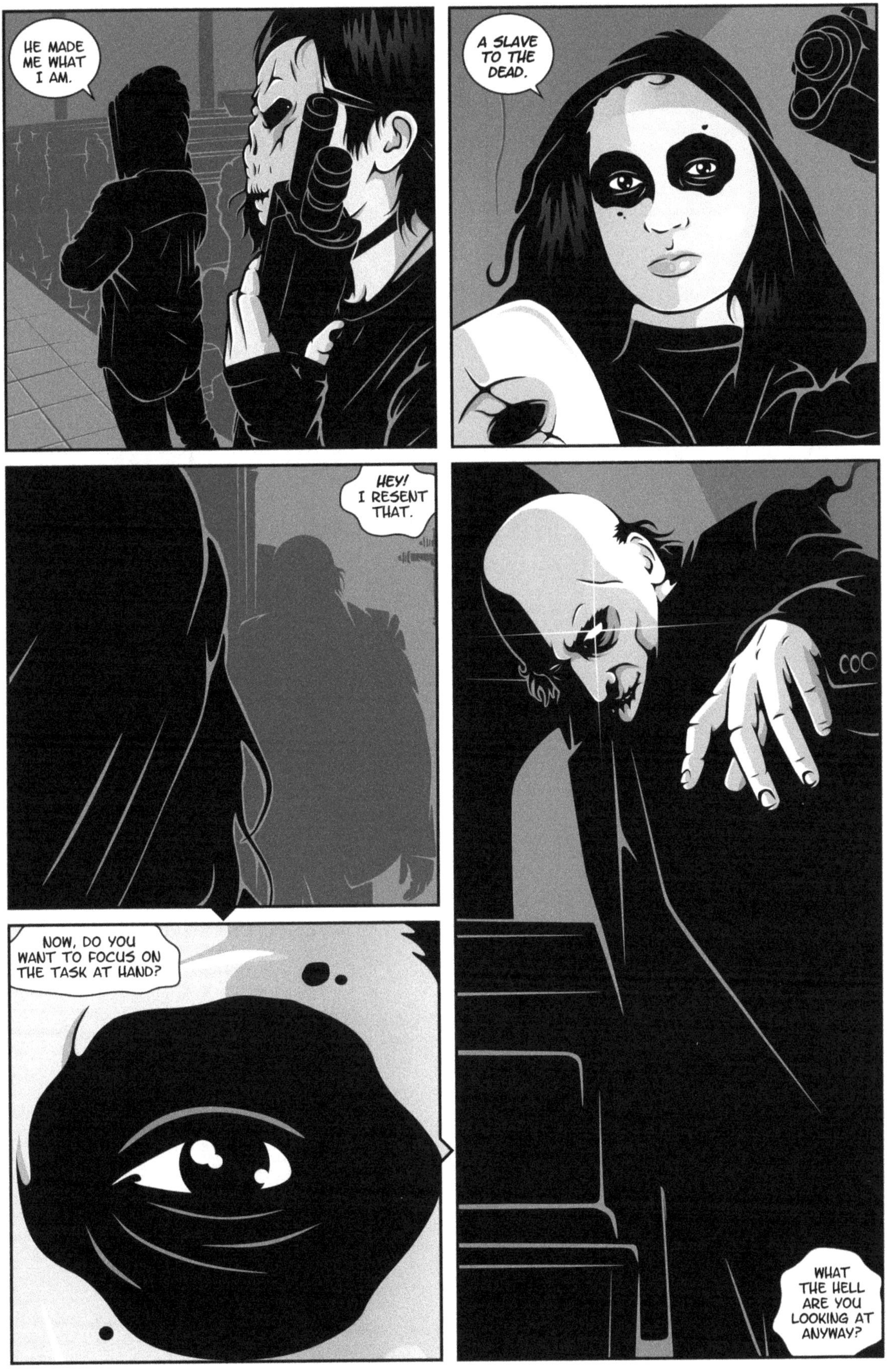
HE MADE ME WHAT I AM.
A SLAVE TO THE DEAD.
HEY! I RESENT THAT.
NOW, DO YOU WANT TO FOCUS ON THE TASK AT HAND?
WHAT THE HELL ARE YOU LOOKING AT ANYWAY?

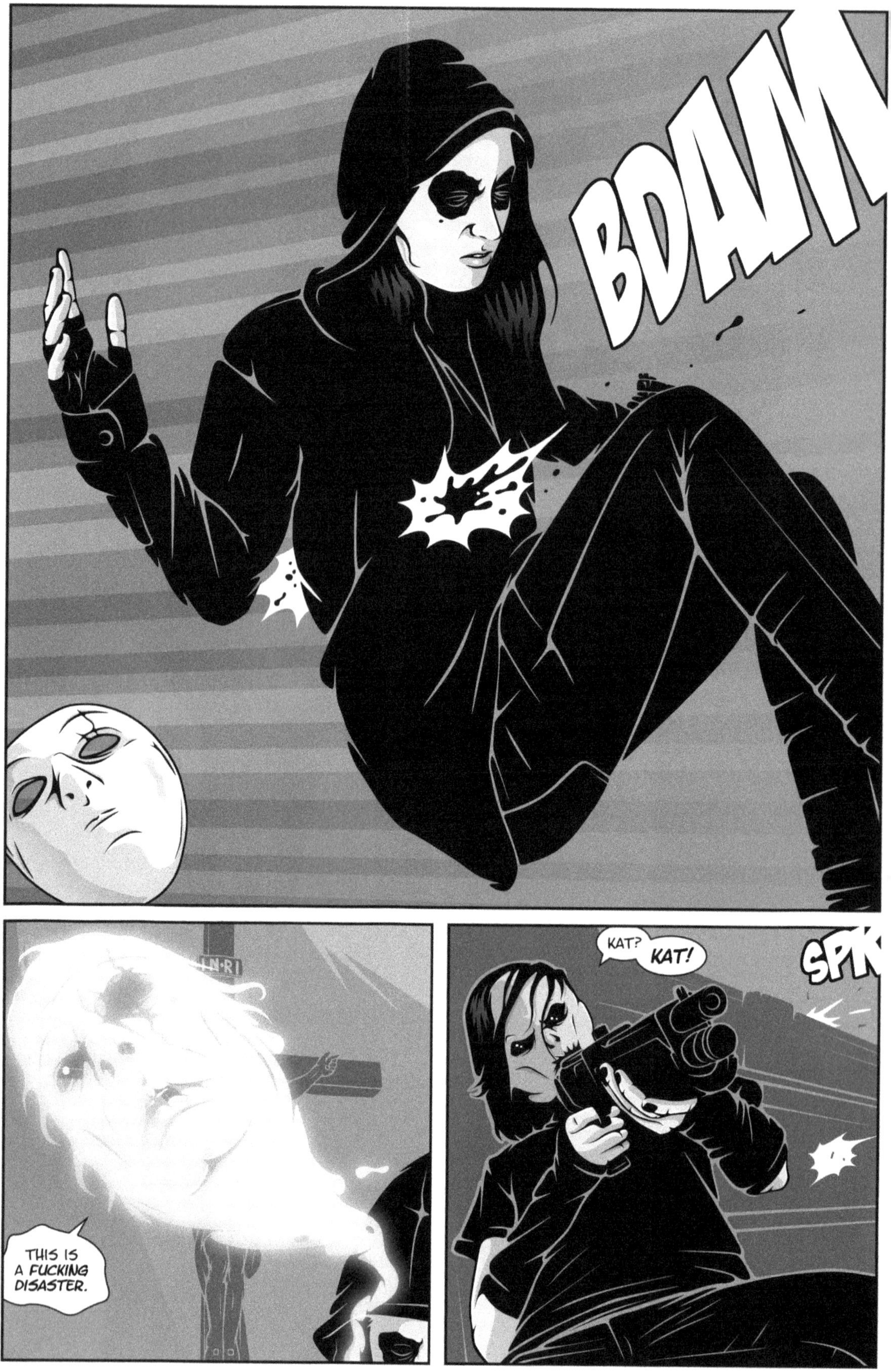
BDAM
THIS IS A FUCKING DISASTER.
KAT?
KAT!

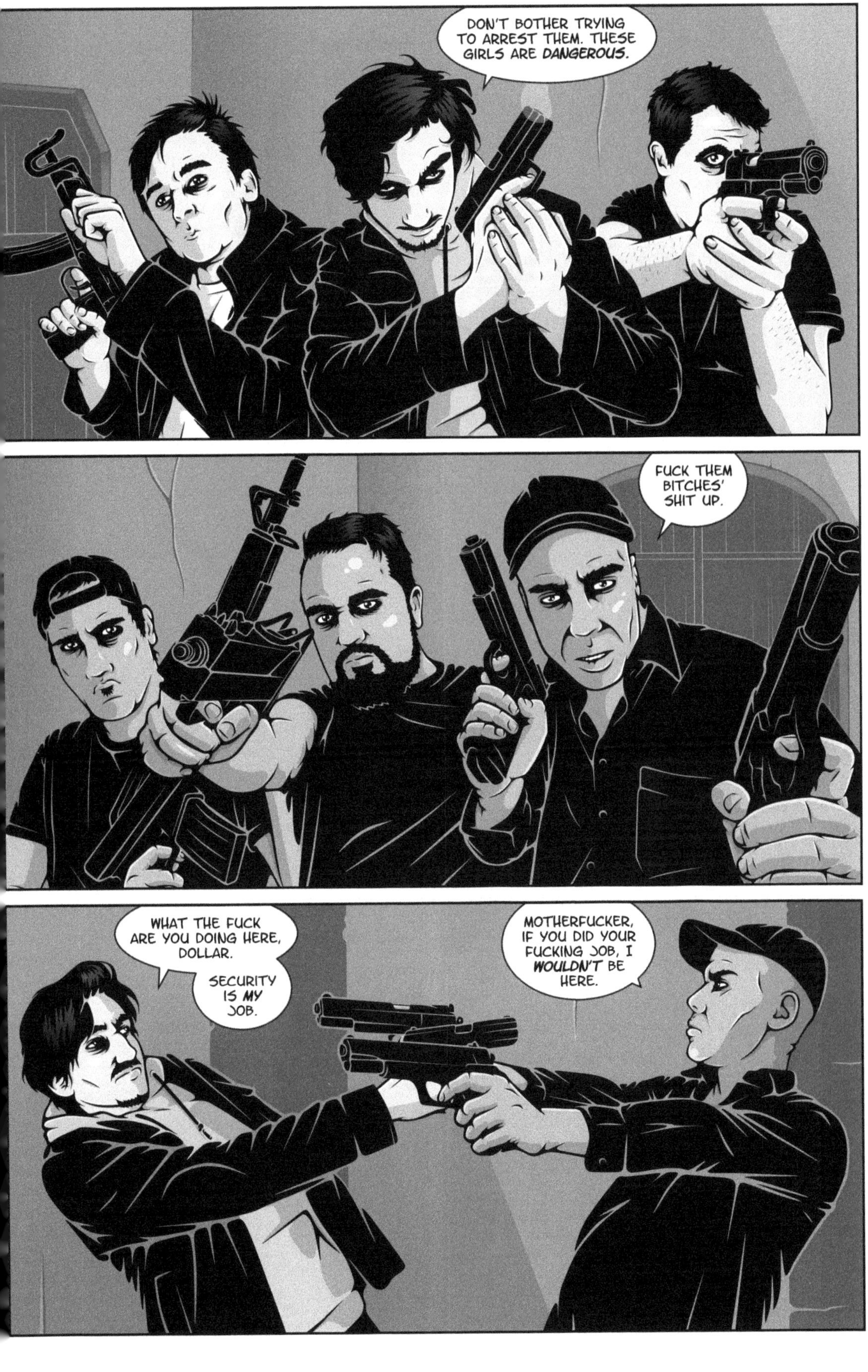
DON'T BOTHER TRYING TO ARREST THEM. THESE GIRLS ARE *DANGEROUS.*
FUCK THEM BITCHES' SHIT UP.
WHAT THE FUCK ARE YOU DOING HERE, DOLLAR.
SECURITY IS *MY* JOB.
MOTHERFUCKER, IF YOU DID YOUR FUCKING JOB, I *WOULDN'T* BE HERE.

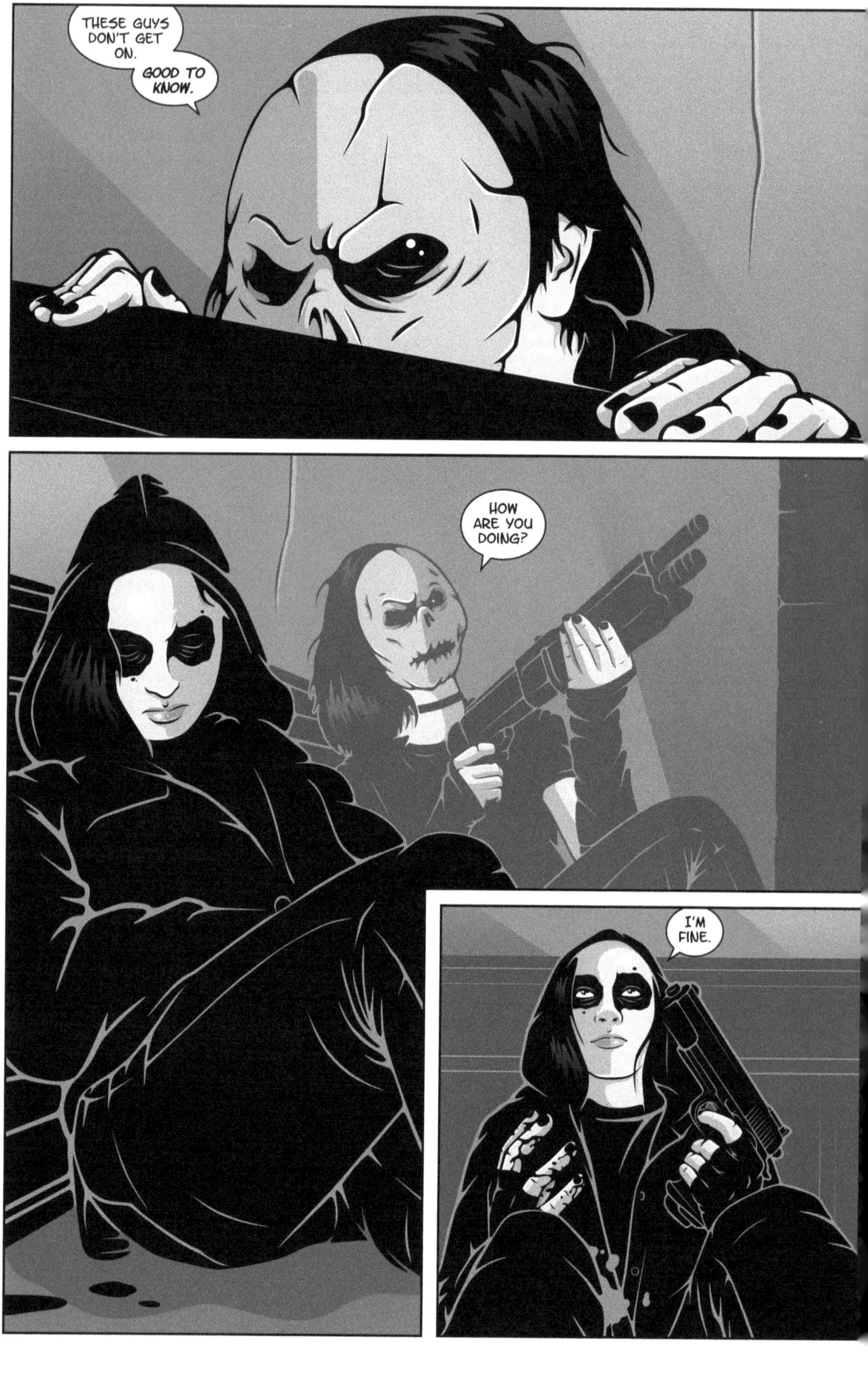
THESE GUYS DON'T GET ON.
GOOD TO KNOW.
HOW ARE YOU DOING?
I'M FINE.

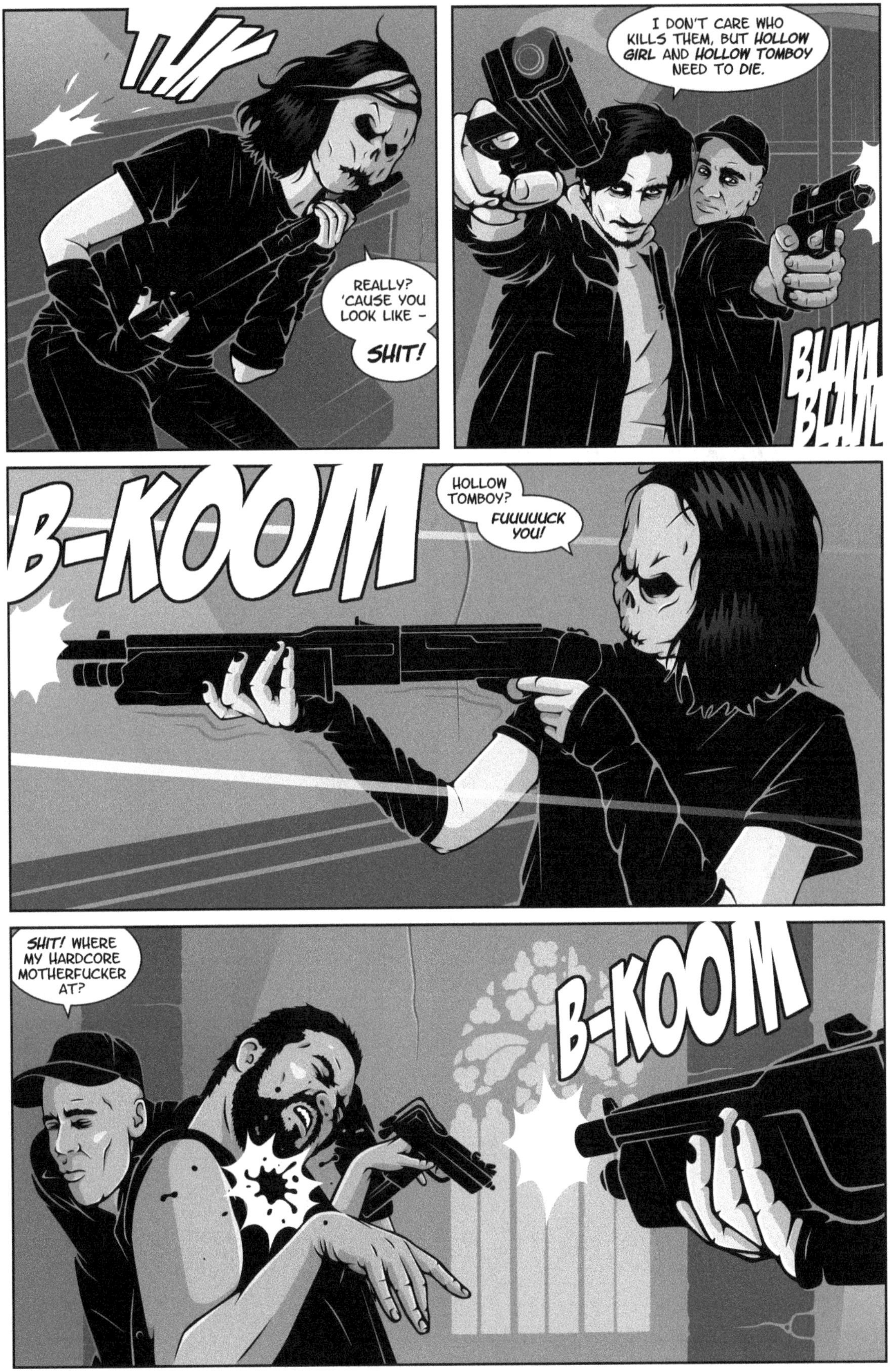
THK
REALLY? 'CAUSE YOU LOOK LIKE –
SHIT!
I DON'T CARE WHO KILLS THEM, BUT HOLLOW GIRL AND HOLLOW TOMBOY NEED TO DIE.
BLAM
BLAM
B-KOOM
HOLLOW TOMBOY?
FUUUUUCK YOU!
SHIT! WHERE MY HARDCORE MOTHERFUCKER AT?
B-KOOM

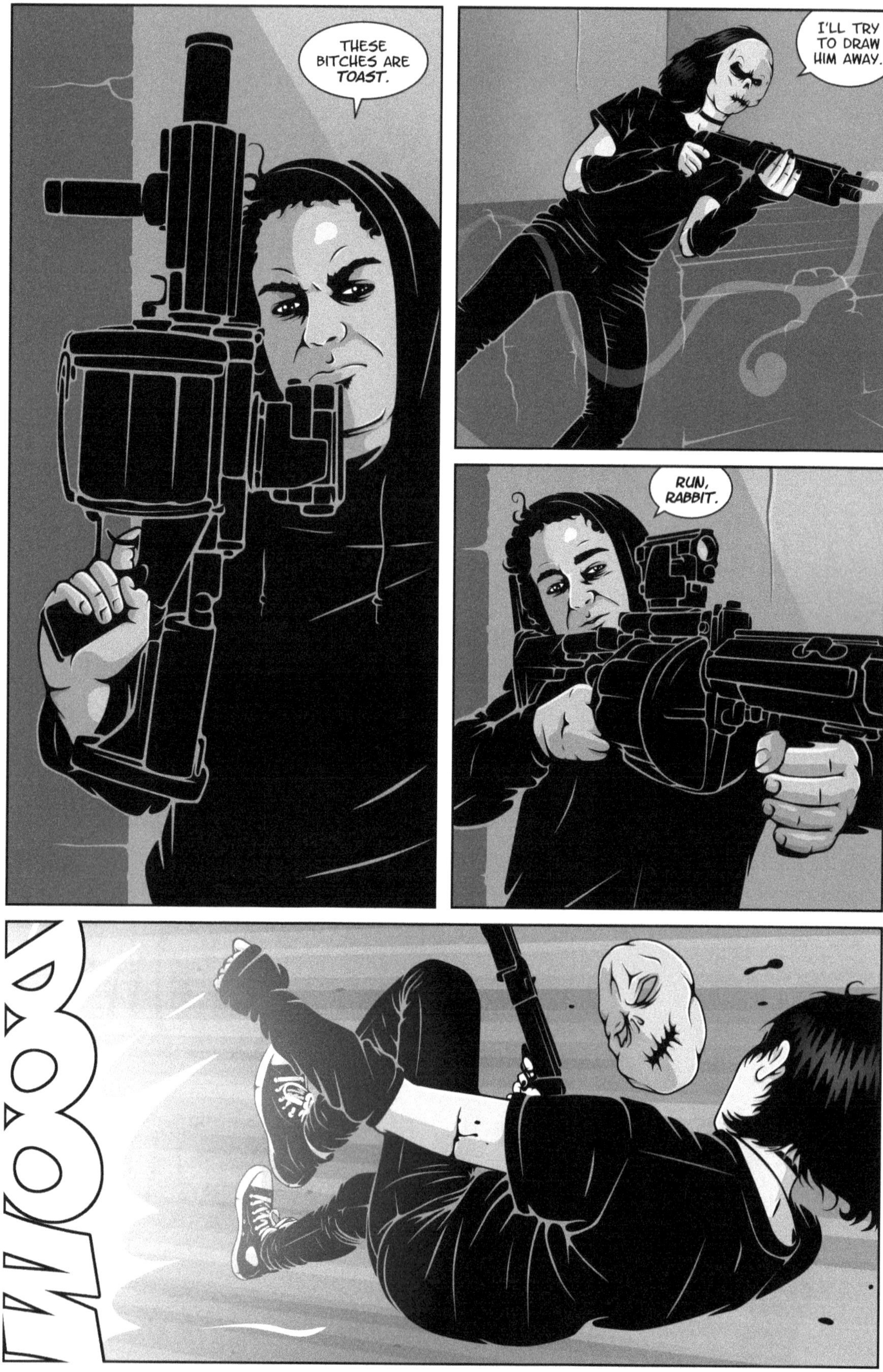
THESE BITCHES ARE TOAST.
I'LL TRY TO DRAW HIM AWAY.
RUN, RABBIT.
BOOM

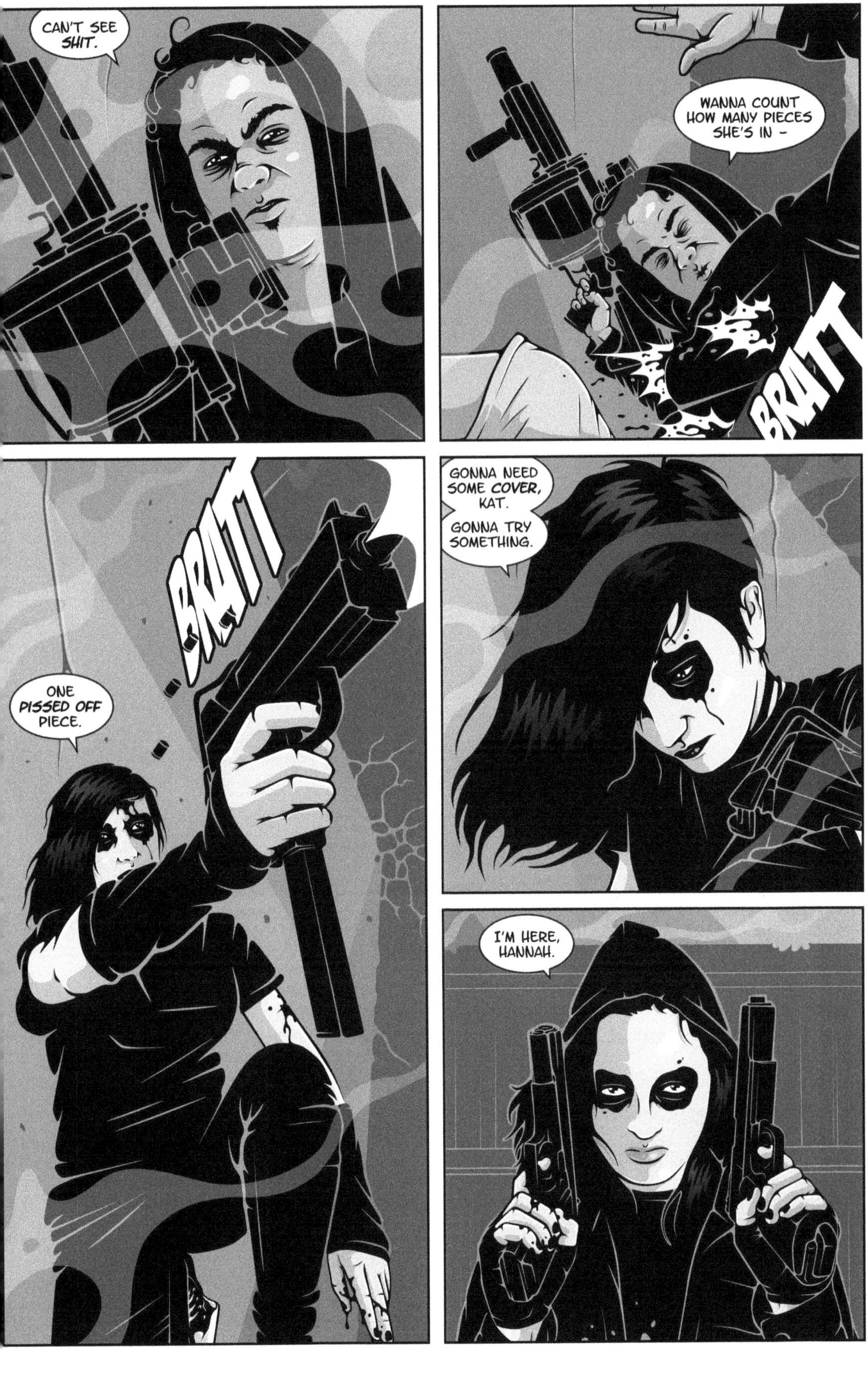
CAN'T SEE SHIT.
WANNA COUNT HOW MANY PIECES SHE'S IN -
BRATT
BRATT
ONE PISSED OFF PIECE.
GONNA NEED SOME COVER, KAT.
GONNA TRY SOMETHING.
I'M HERE, HANNAH.

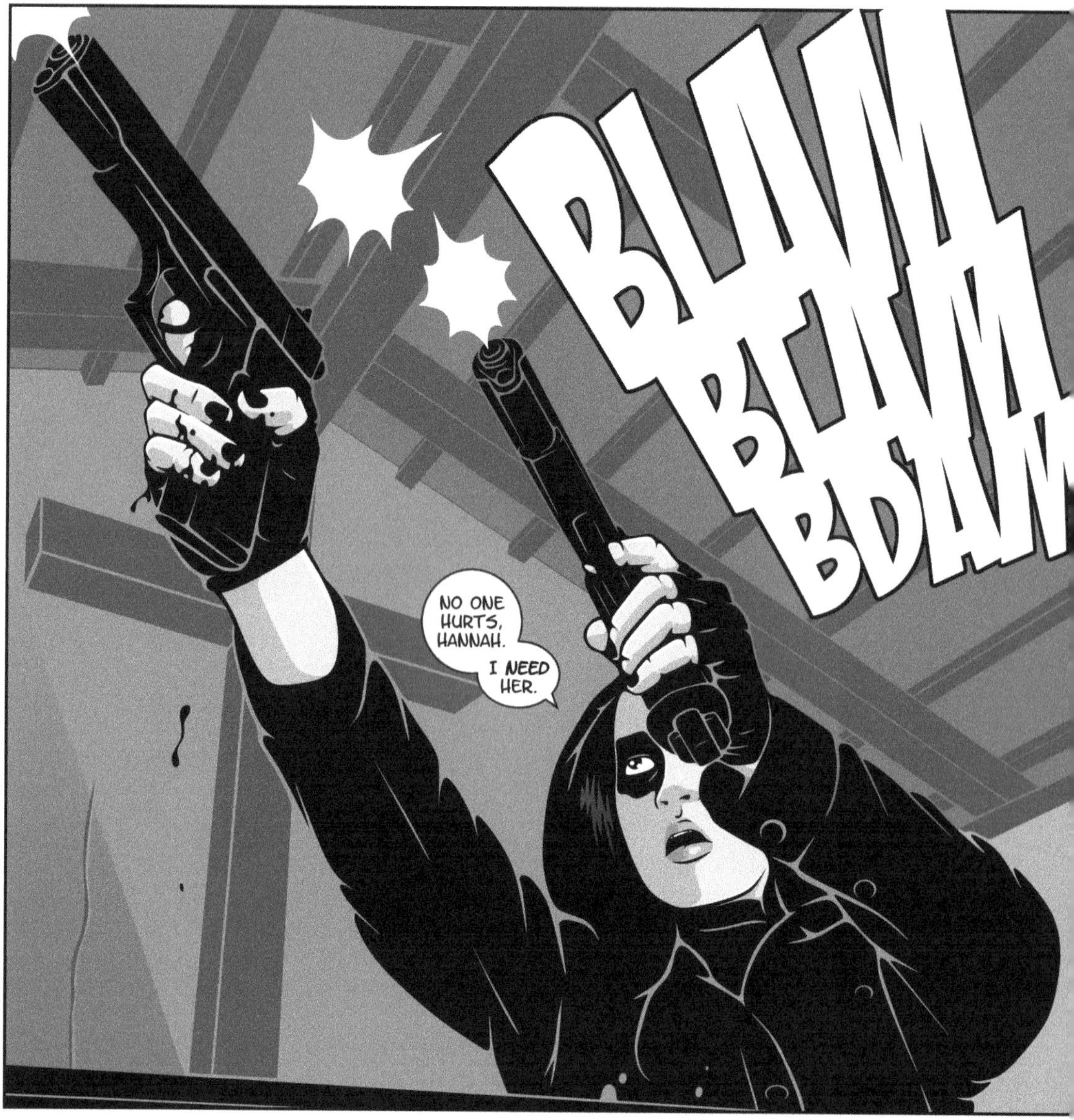
BLAM
BLAM
BLAM
NO ONE HURTS, HANNAH.
I NEED HER.

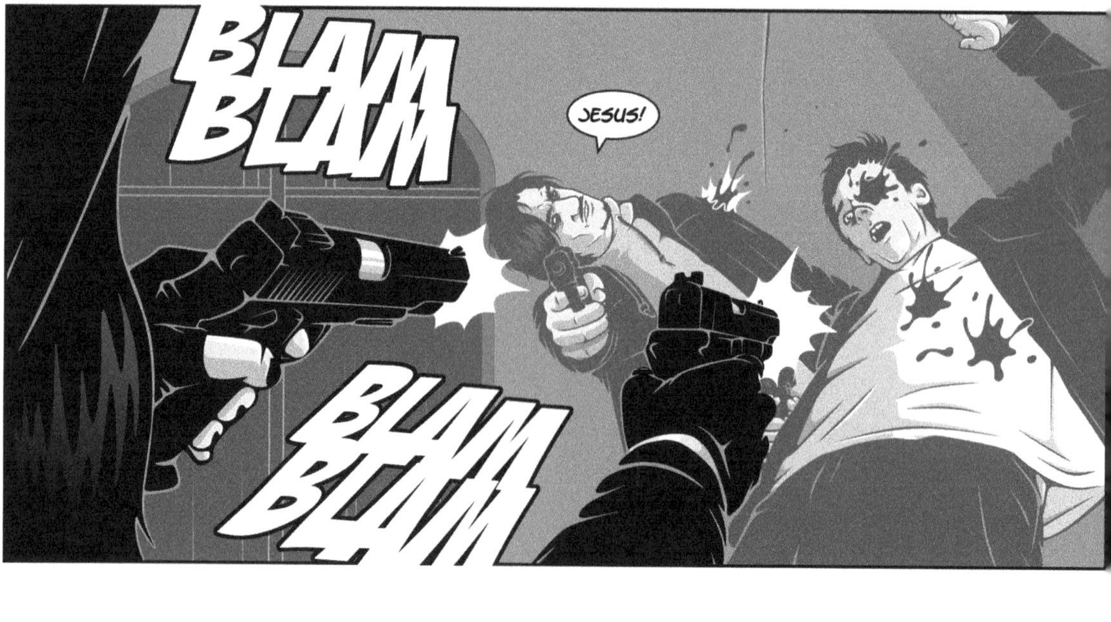
BLAM
BLAM
JESUS!
BLAM
BLAM

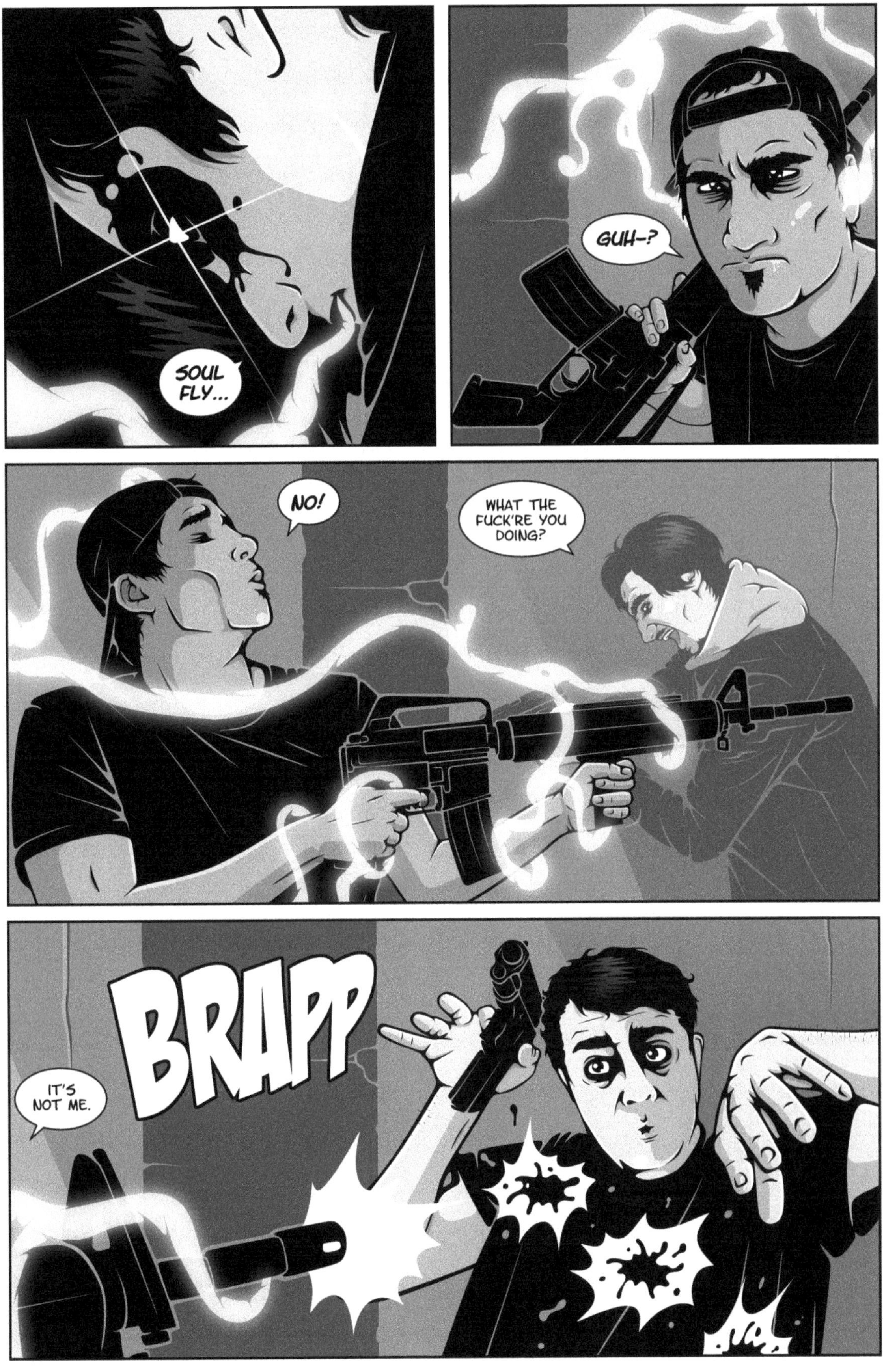
SOUL FLY...
GUH-?
NO!
WHAT THE FUCK'RE YOU DOING?
BRAPP
IT'S NOT ME.

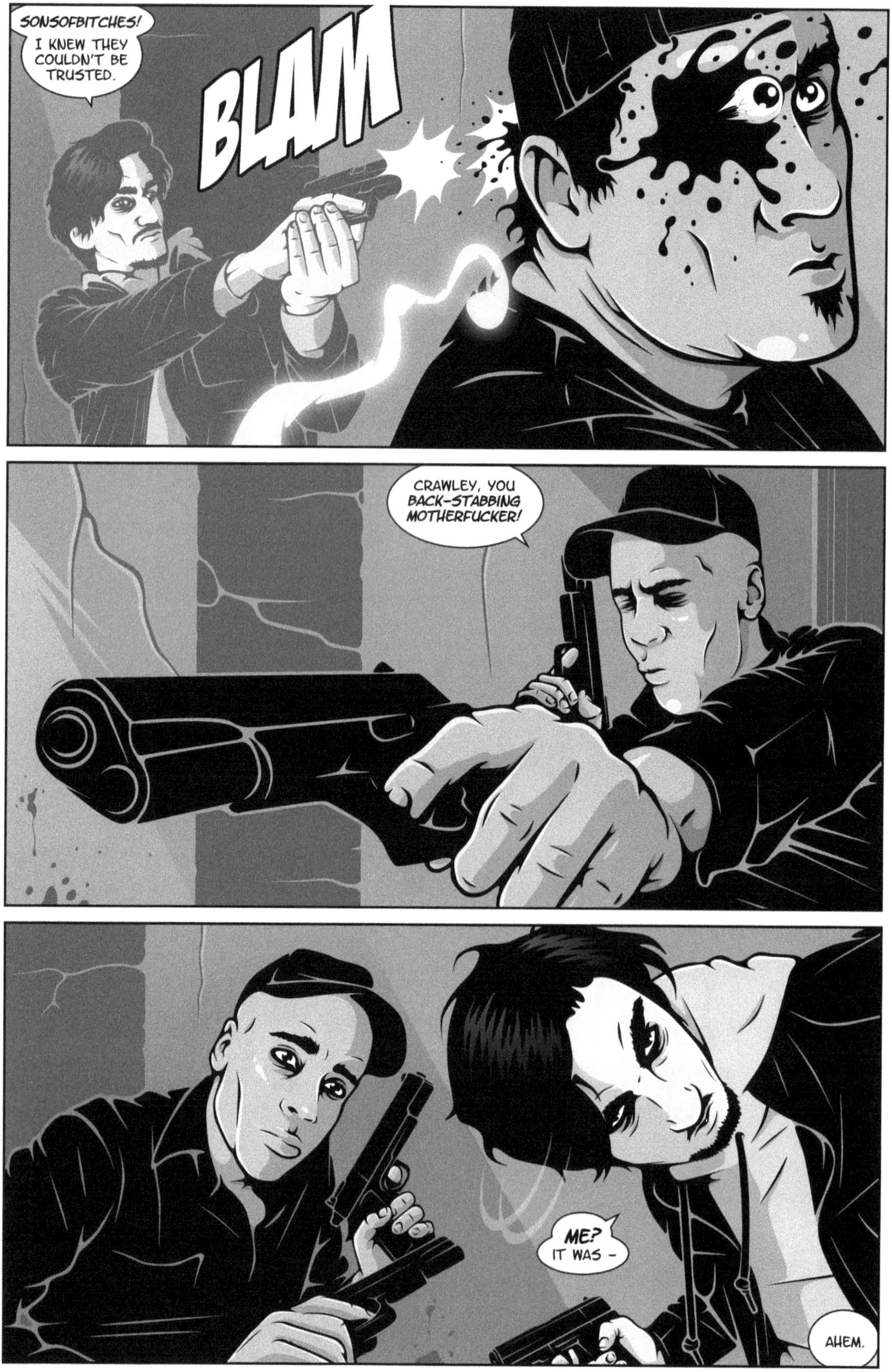
SONSOFBITCHES!
I KNEW THEY COULDN'T BE TRUSTED.
BLAM
CRAWLEY, YOU BACK-STABBING MOTHERFUCKER!
ME? IT WAS –
AHEM.

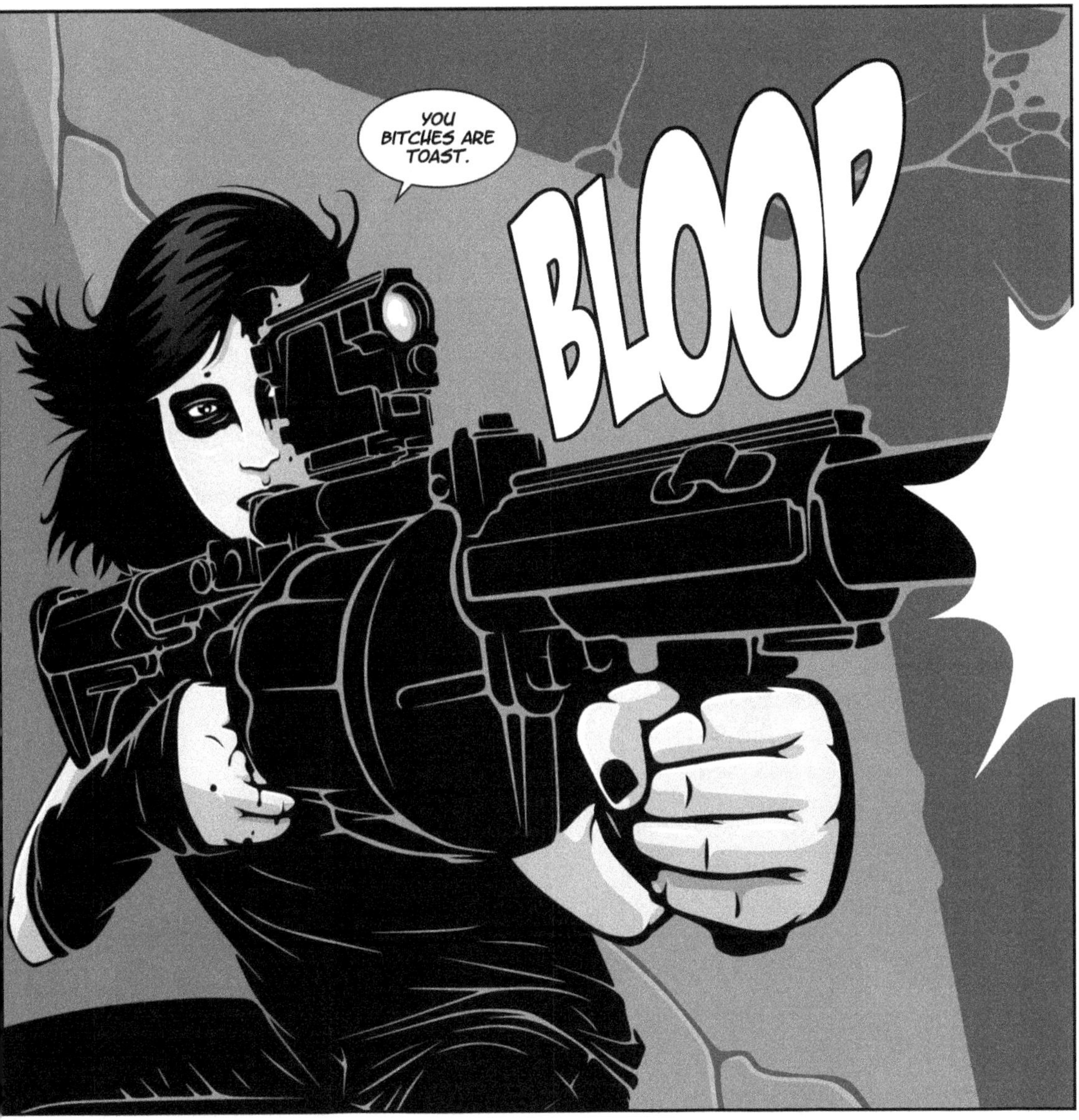
YOU BITCHES ARE TOAST.
BLOOP
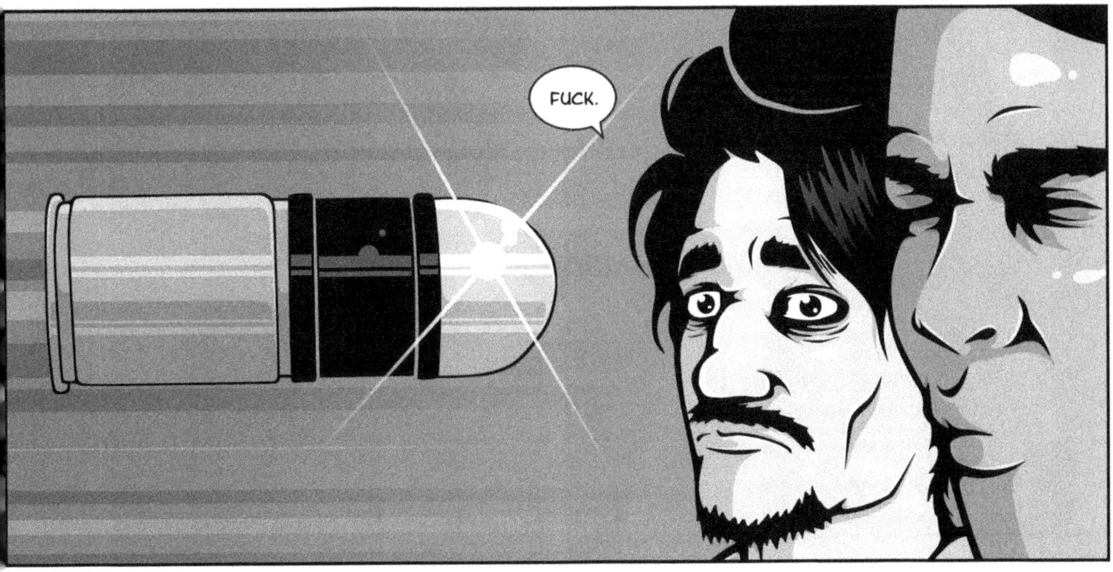
FUCK.

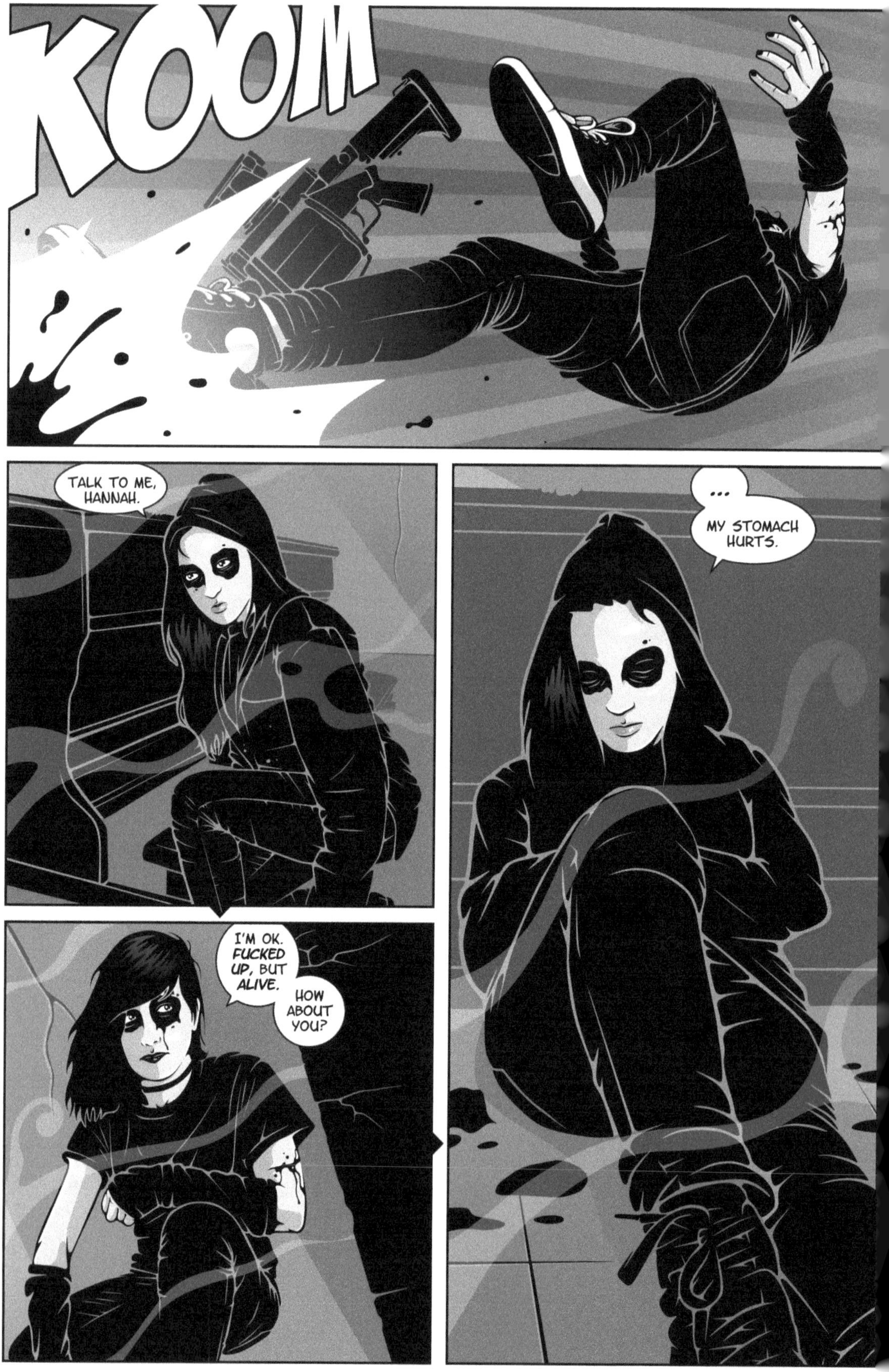
KOOM
TALK TO ME, HANNAH.
...
MY STOMACH HURTS.
I'M OK. **FUCKED UP**, BUT **ALIVE**.
HOW ABOUT YOU?

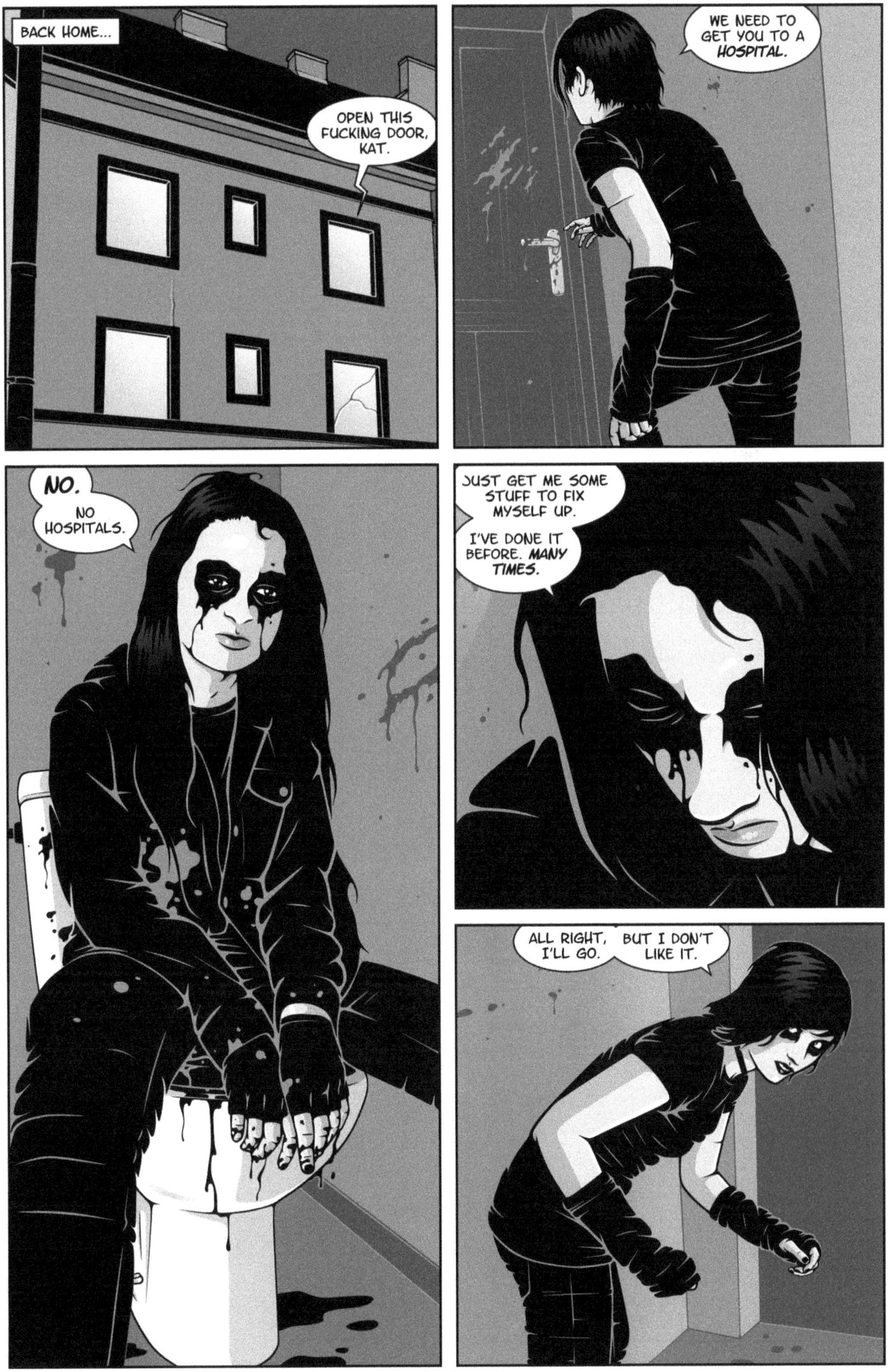
BACK HOME...
OPEN THIS FUCKING DOOR, KAT.
WE NEED TO GET YOU TO A **HOSPITAL.**
NO.
NO HOSPITALS.
JUST GET ME SOME STUFF TO FIX MYSELF UP.
I'VE DONE IT BEFORE. ***MANY TIMES.***
ALL RIGHT, I'LL GO.
BUT I DON'T LIKE IT.

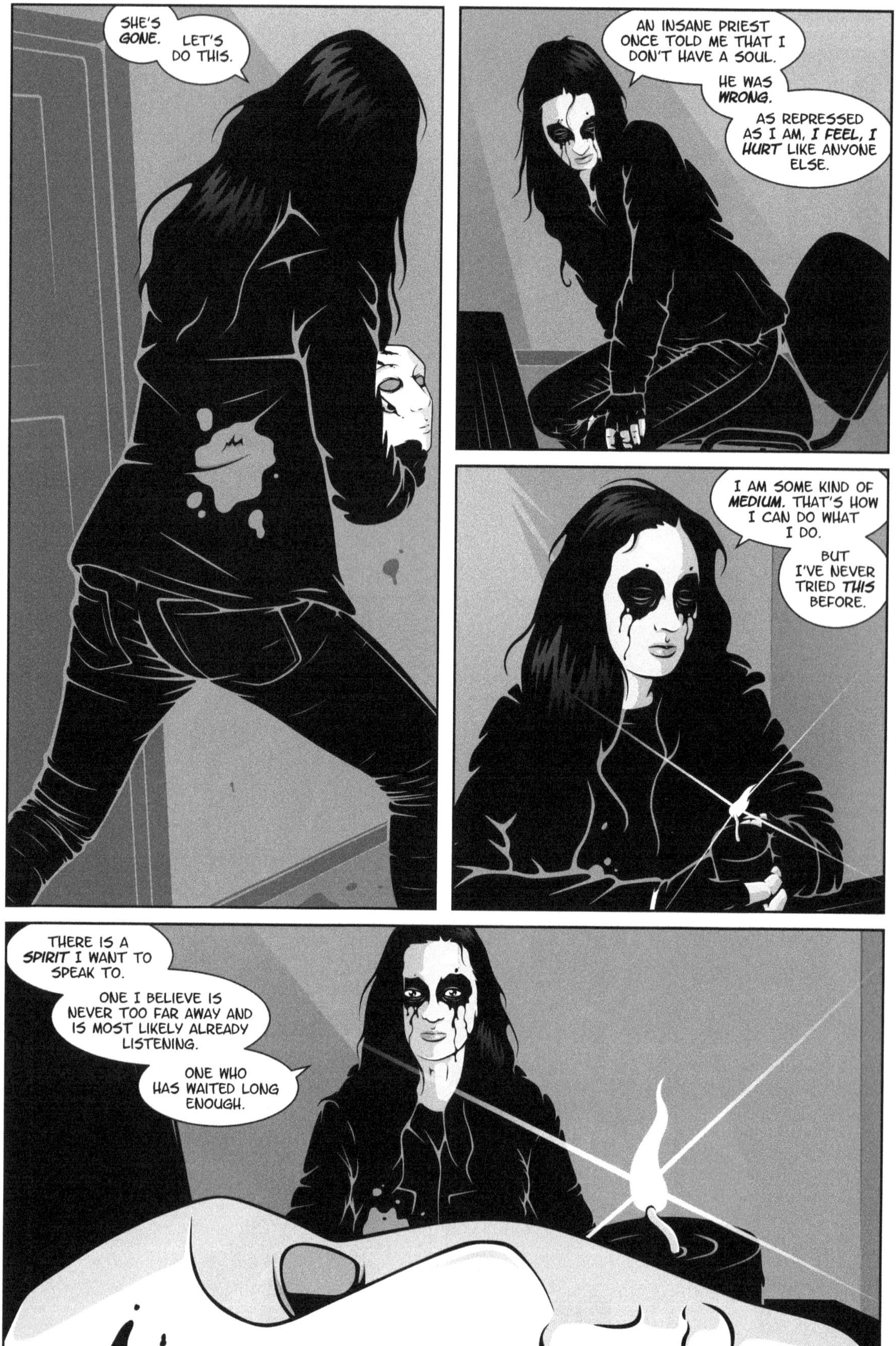
SHE'S *GONE.*
LET'S DO THIS.
AN INSANE PRIEST ONCE TOLD ME THAT I DON'T HAVE A SOUL.
HE WAS *WRONG.*
AS REPRESSED AS I AM, *I FEEL, I HURT* LIKE ANYONE ELSE.
I AM SOME KIND OF *MEDIUM.* THAT'S HOW I CAN DO WHAT I DO.
BUT I'VE NEVER TRIED *THIS* BEFORE.
THERE IS A *SPIRIT* I WANT TO SPEAK TO.
ONE I BELIEVE IS NEVER TOO FAR AWAY AND IS MOST LIKELY ALREADY LISTENING.
ONE WHO HAS WAITED LONG ENOUGH.

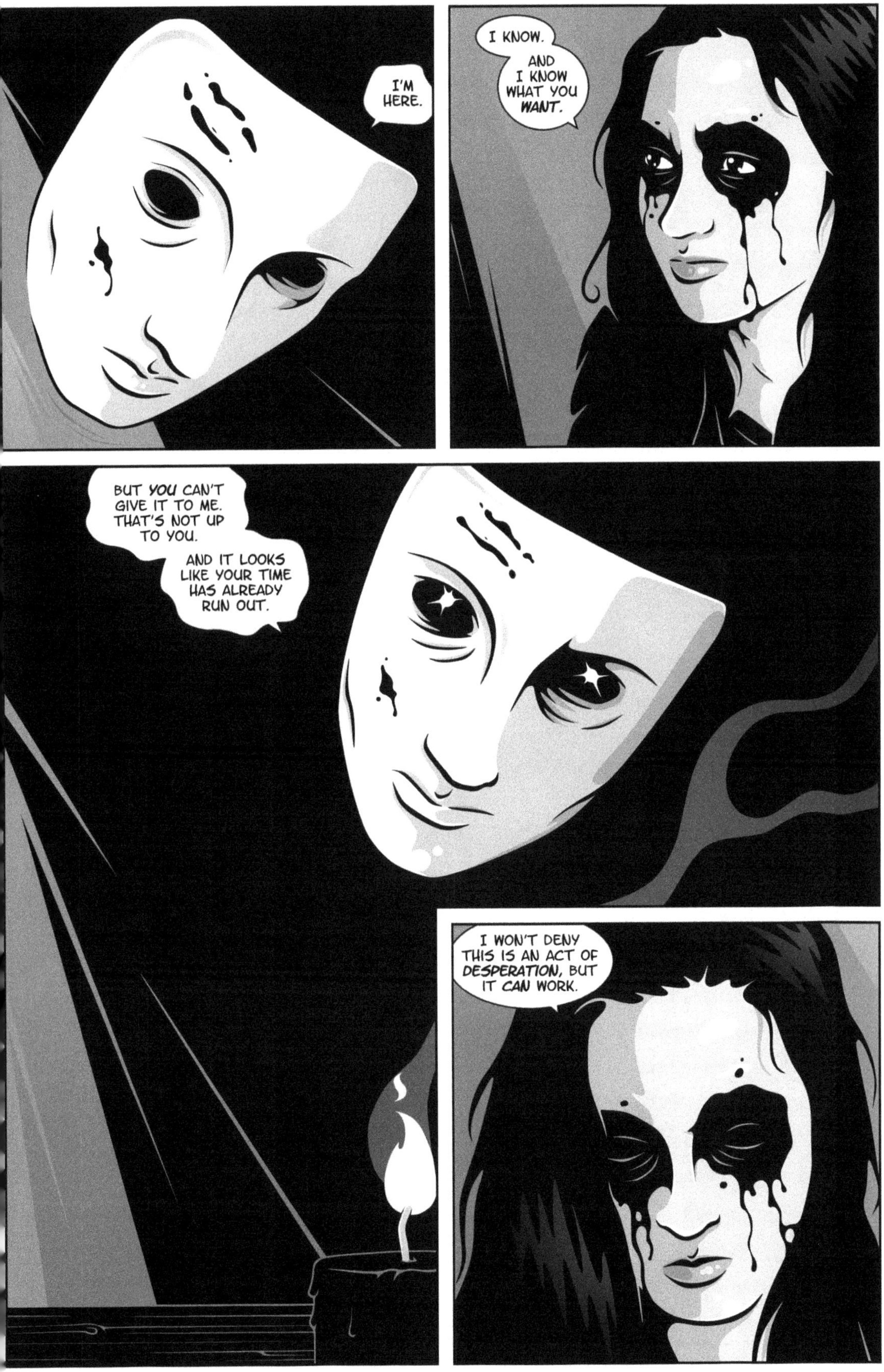
I'M HERE.
I KNOW.
AND I KNOW WHAT YOU WANT.
BUT YOU CAN'T GIVE IT TO ME. THAT'S NOT UP TO YOU.
AND IT LOOKS LIKE YOUR TIME HAS ALREADY RUN OUT.
I WON'T DENY THIS IS AN ACT OF DESPERATION, BUT IT CAN WORK.

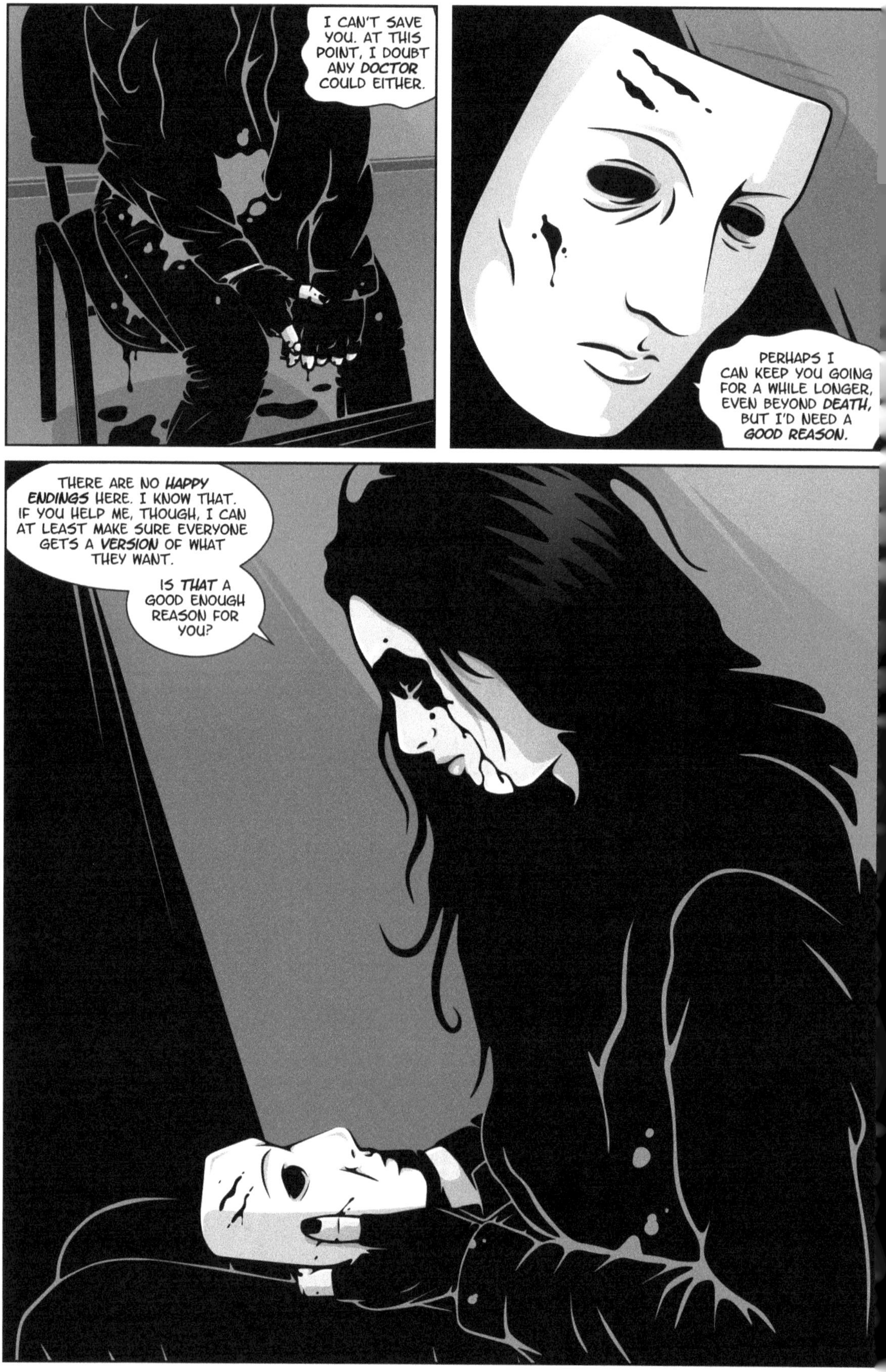
I CAN'T SAVE YOU. AT THIS POINT, I DOUBT ANY DOCTOR COULD EITHER.
PERHAPS I CAN KEEP YOU GOING FOR A WHILE LONGER, EVEN BEYOND DEATH, BUT I'D NEED A GOOD REASON.
THERE ARE NO HAPPY ENDINGS HERE. I KNOW THAT. IF YOU HELP ME, THOUGH, I CAN AT LEAST MAKE SURE EVERYONE GETS A VERSION OF WHAT THEY WANT.
IS THAT A GOOD ENOUGH REASON FOR YOU?

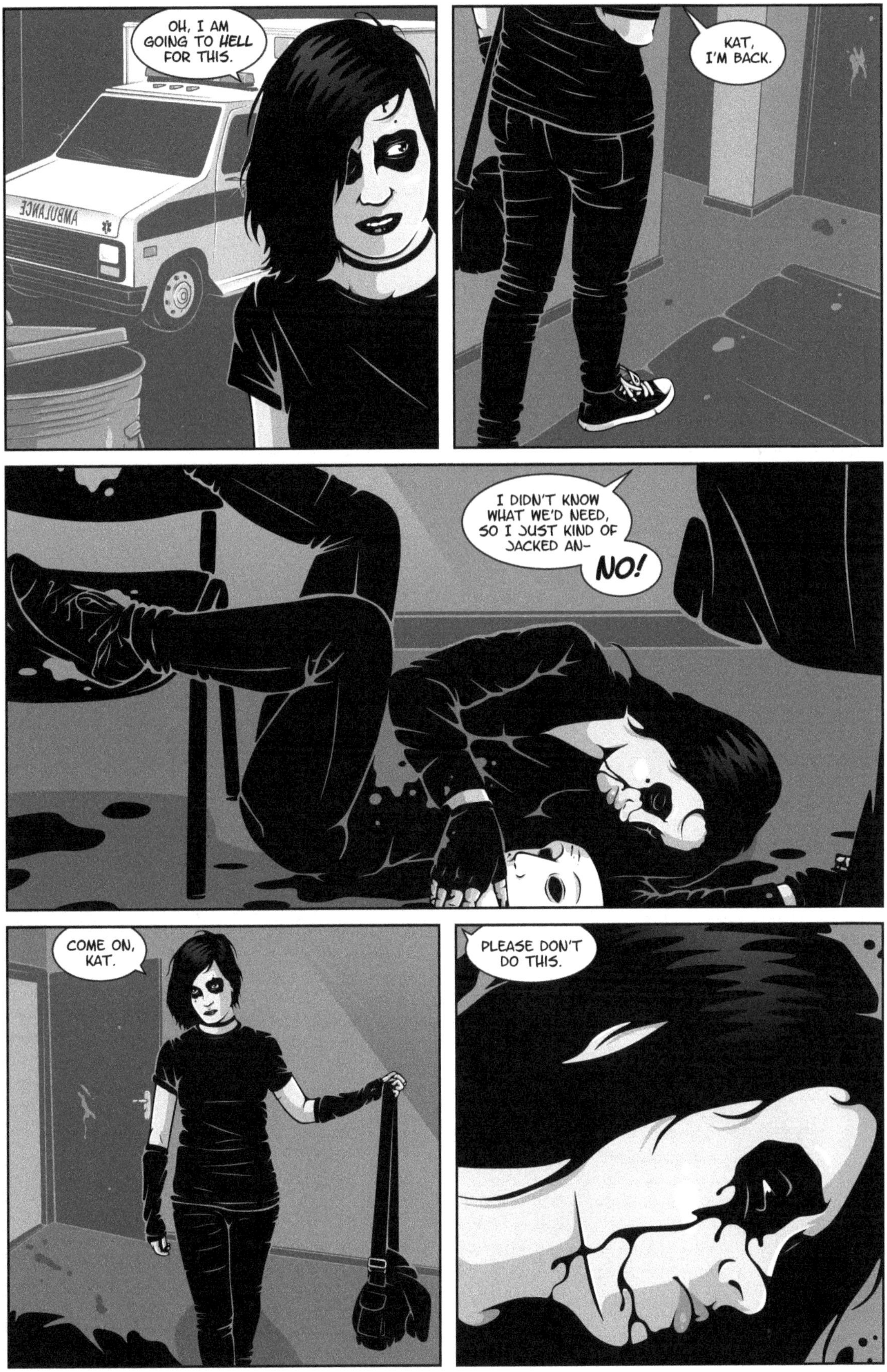
OH, I AM GOING TO HELL FOR THIS.
KAT, I'M BACK.
I DIDN'T KNOW WHAT WE'D NEED, SO I JUST KIND OF JACKED AN-
NO!
COME ON, KAT.
PLEASE DON'T DO THIS.
AMBULANCE

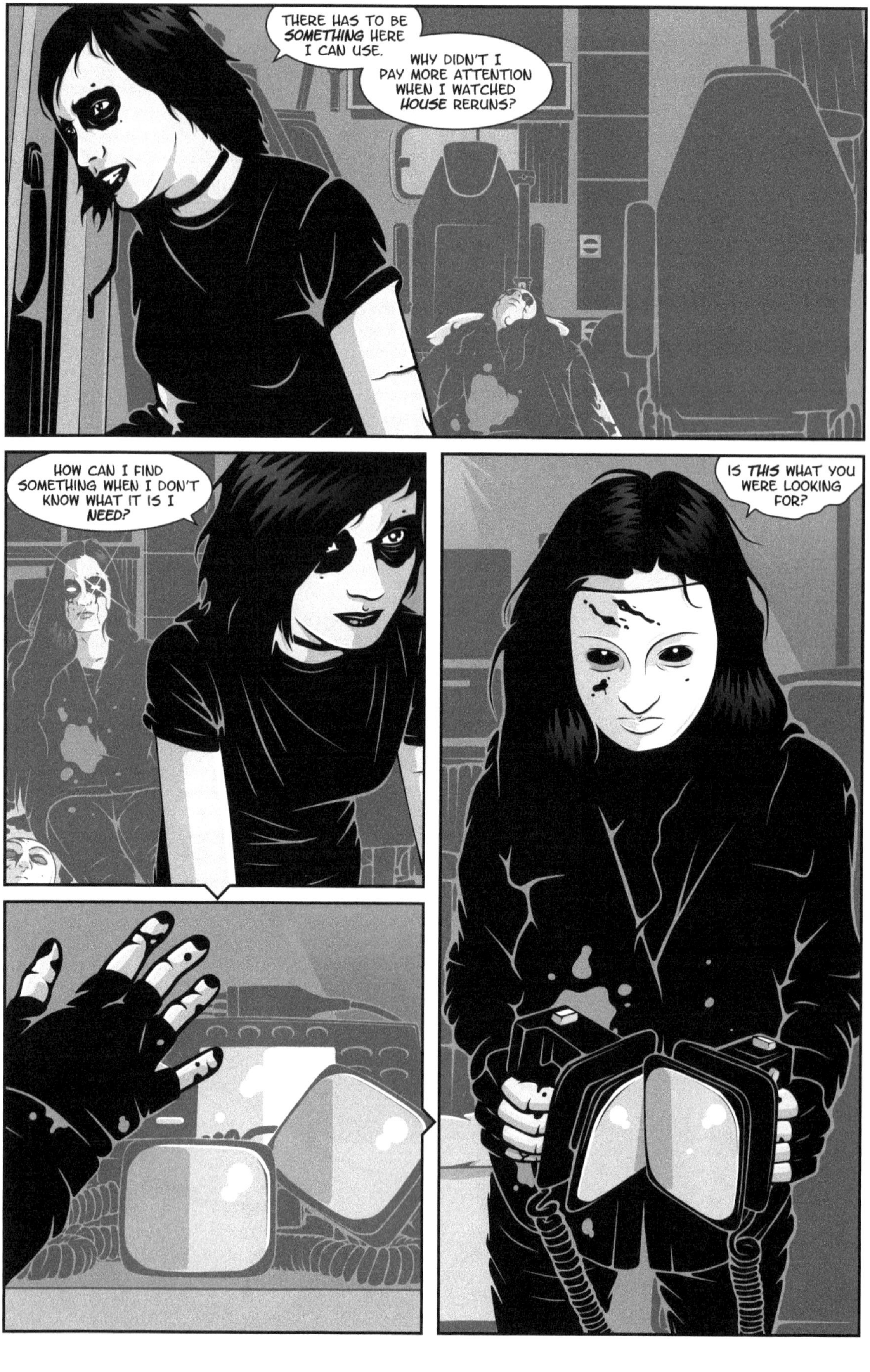
THERE HAS TO BE SOMETHING HERE I CAN USE.
WHY DIDN'T I PAY MORE ATTENTION WHEN I WATCHED HOUSE RERUNS?
HOW CAN I FIND SOMETHING WHEN I DON'T KNOW WHAT IT IS I NEED?
IS THIS WHAT YOU WERE LOOKING FOR?

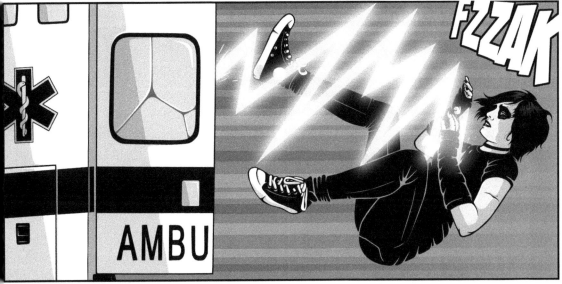

FZZAK

AMBU

I'M SORRY...

KAT! WHAT THE FUCK DID YOU DO?

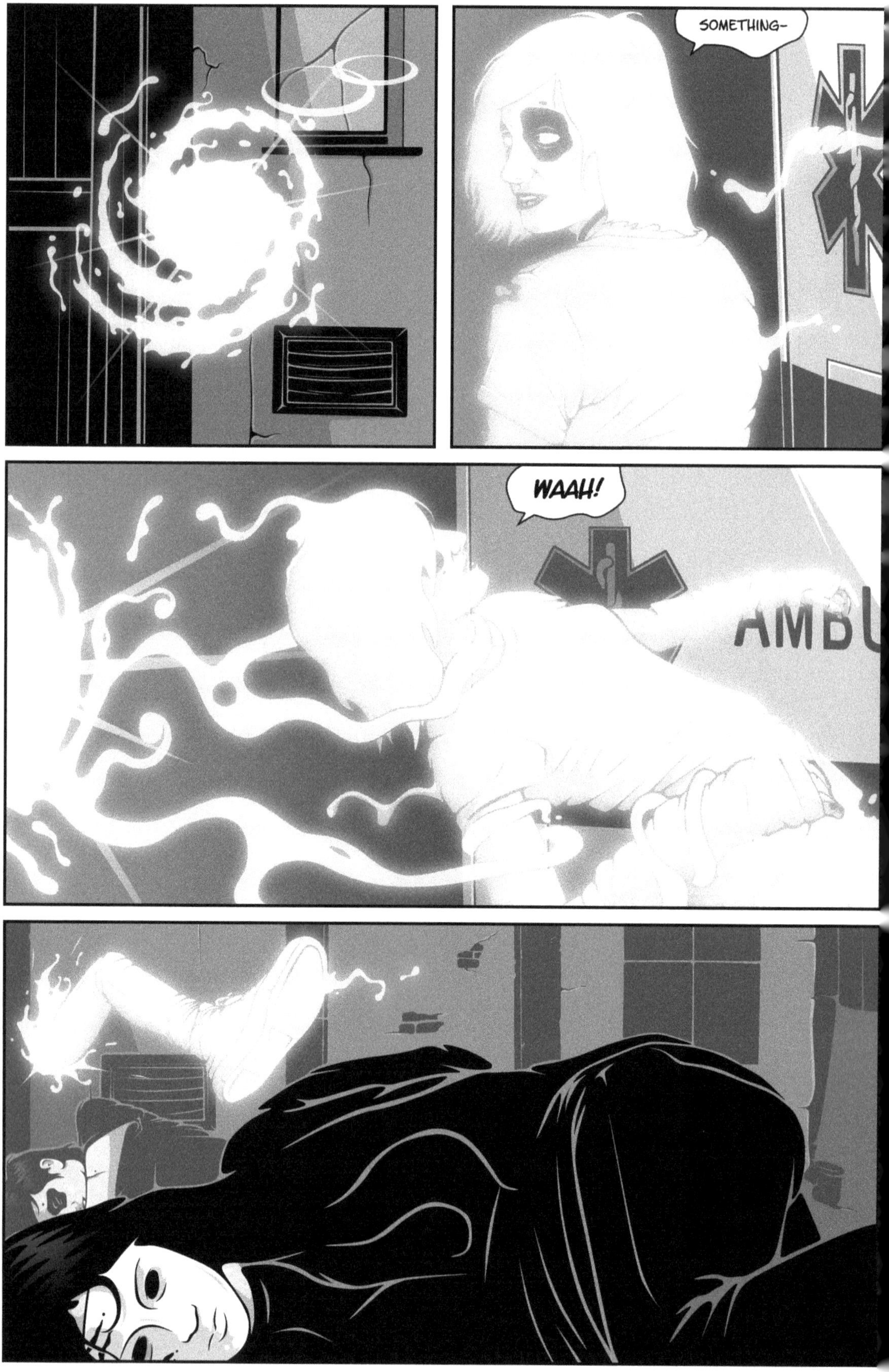
SOMETHING-
WAAH!
AMBU

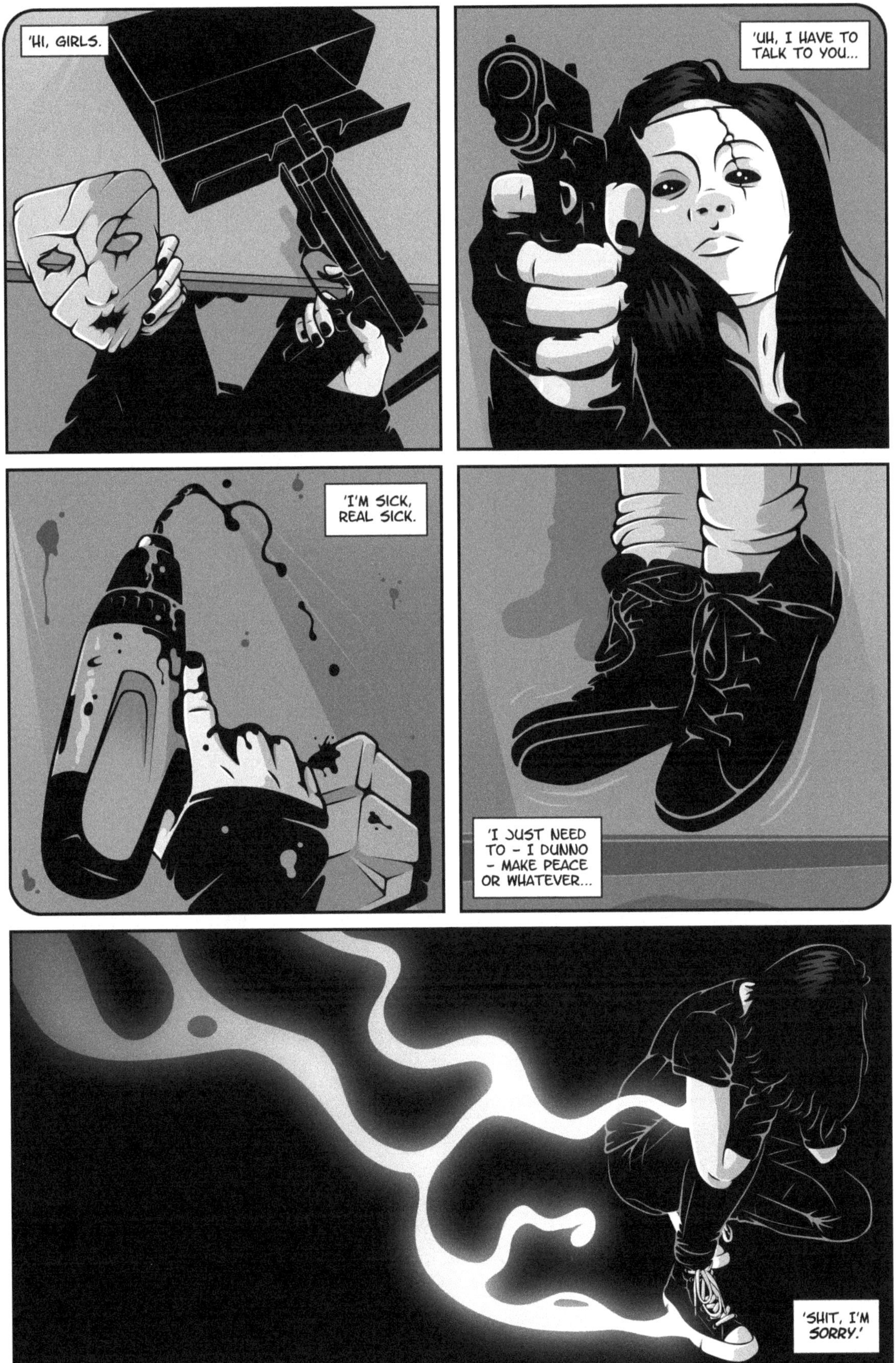
'HI, GIRLS.
'UH, I HAVE TO TALK TO YOU...
'I'M SICK, REAL SICK.
'I JUST NEED TO - I DUNNO - MAKE PEACE OR WHATEVER...
'SHIT, I'M SORRY.'

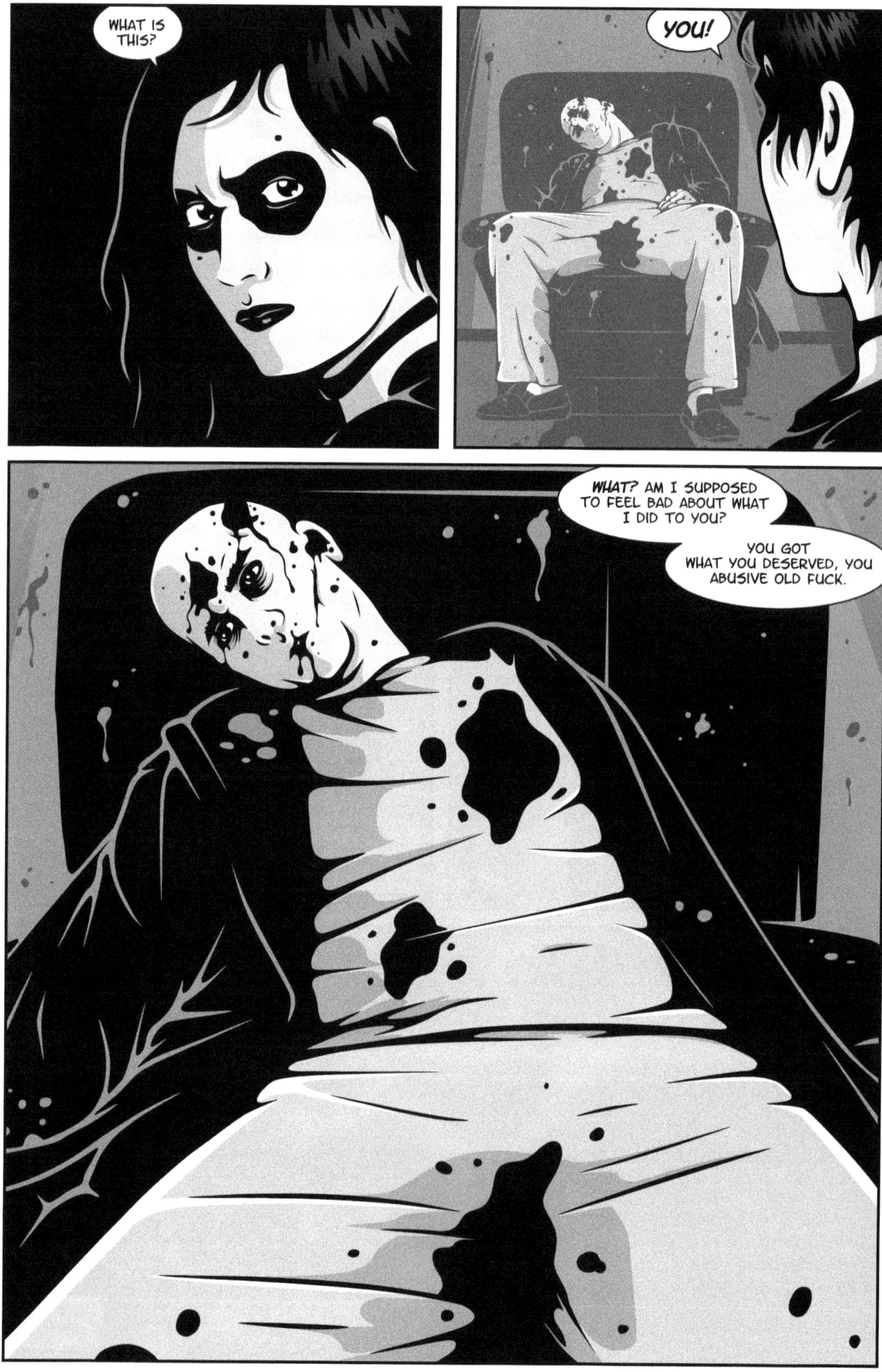
WHAT IS THIS?
YOU!
WHAT? AM I SUPPOSED TO FEEL BAD ABOUT WHAT I DID TO YOU?
YOU GOT WHAT YOU DESERVED, YOU ABUSIVE OLD FUCK.

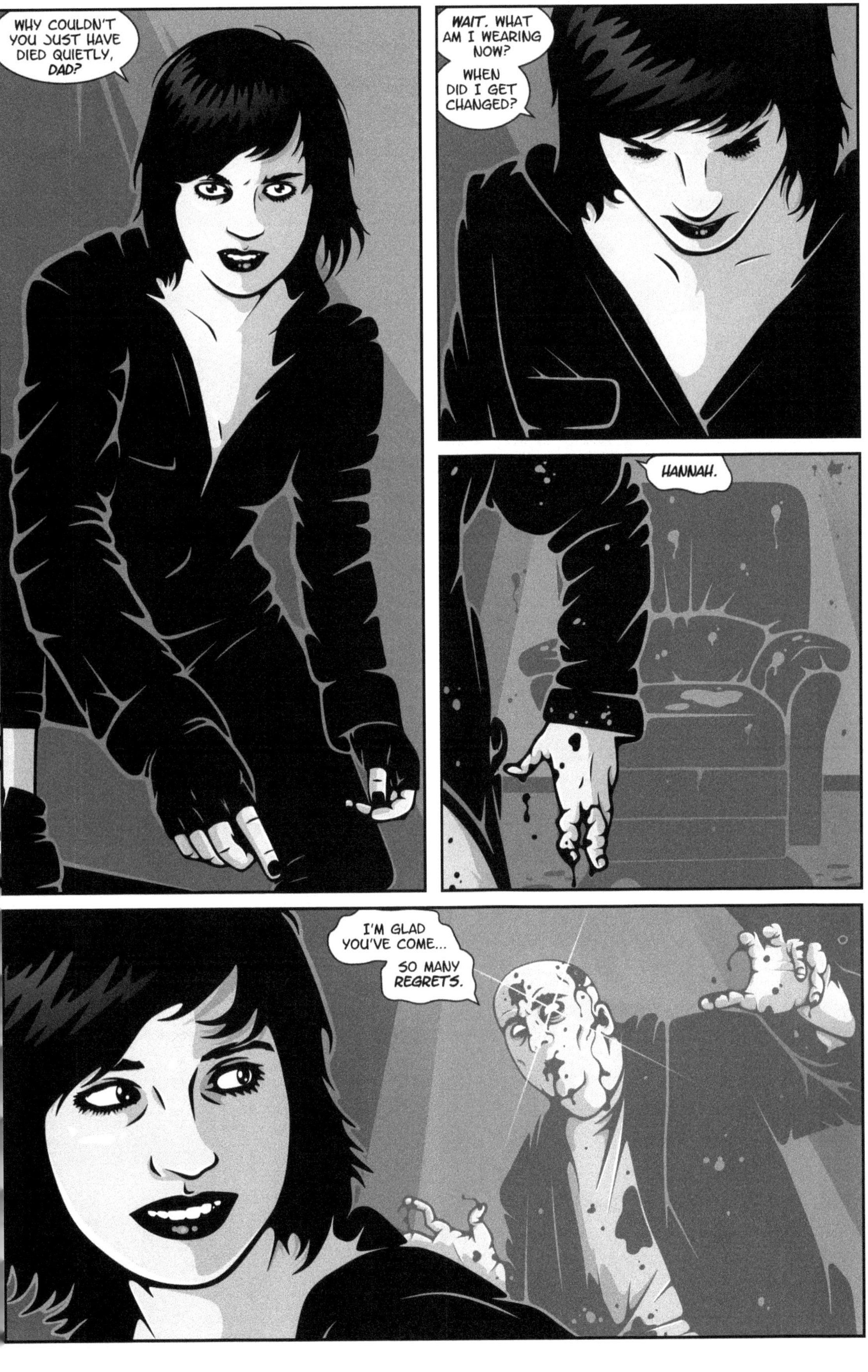
WHY COULDN'T YOU JUST HAVE DIED QUIETLY, DAD?
WAIT. WHAT AM I WEARING NOW?
WHEN DID I GET CHANGED?
HANNAH.
I'M GLAD YOU'VE COME...
SO MANY REGRETS.

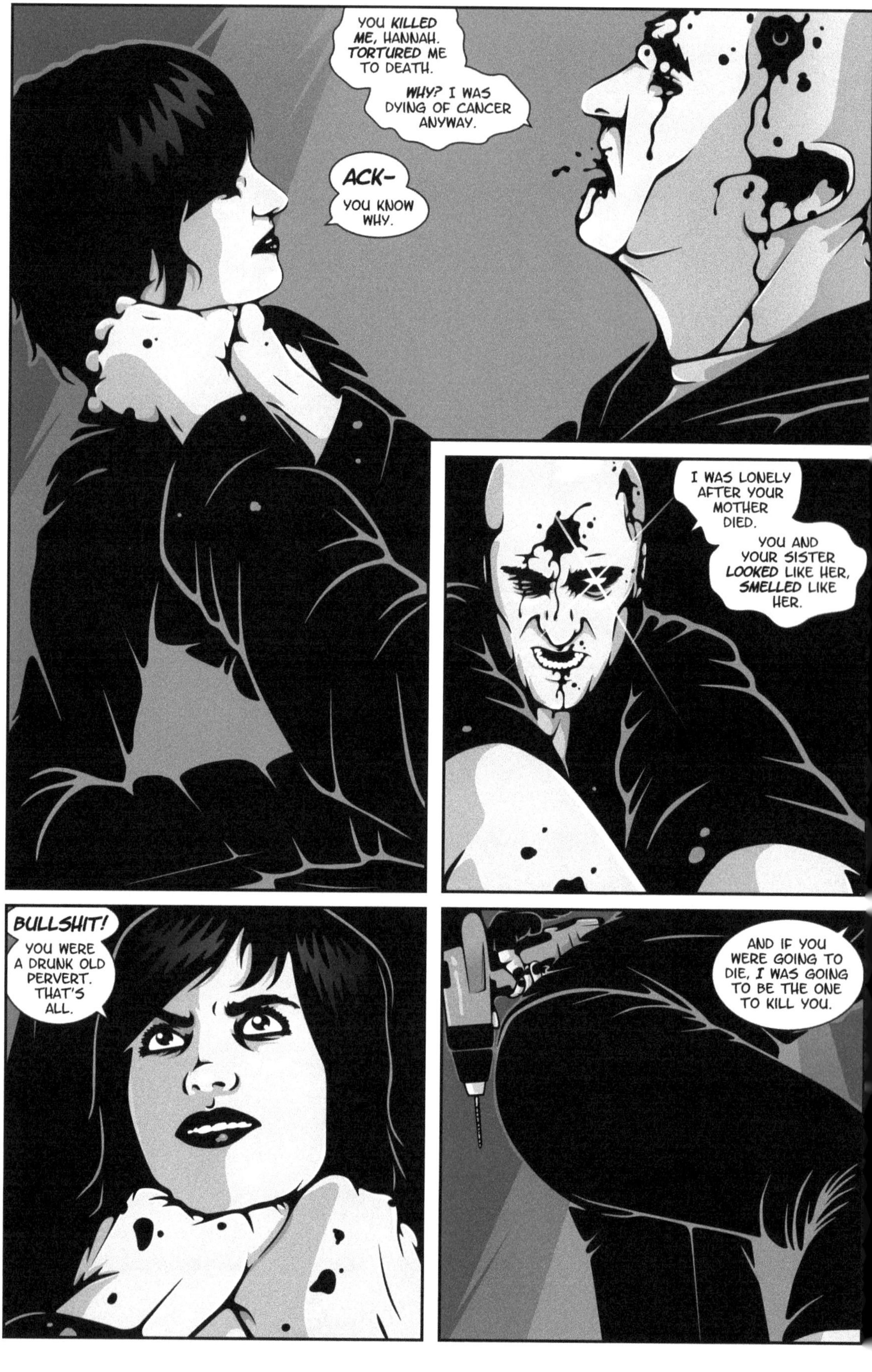
YOU KILLED ME, HANNAH. TORTURED ME TO DEATH.
WHY? I WAS DYING OF CANCER ANYWAY.
ACK-
YOU KNOW WHY.
I WAS LONELY AFTER YOUR MOTHER DIED.
YOU AND YOUR SISTER LOOKED LIKE HER, SMELLED LIKE HER.
BULLSHIT!
YOU WERE A DRUNK OLD PERVERT. THAT'S ALL.
AND IF YOU WERE GOING TO DIE, I WAS GOING TO BE THE ONE TO KILL YOU.

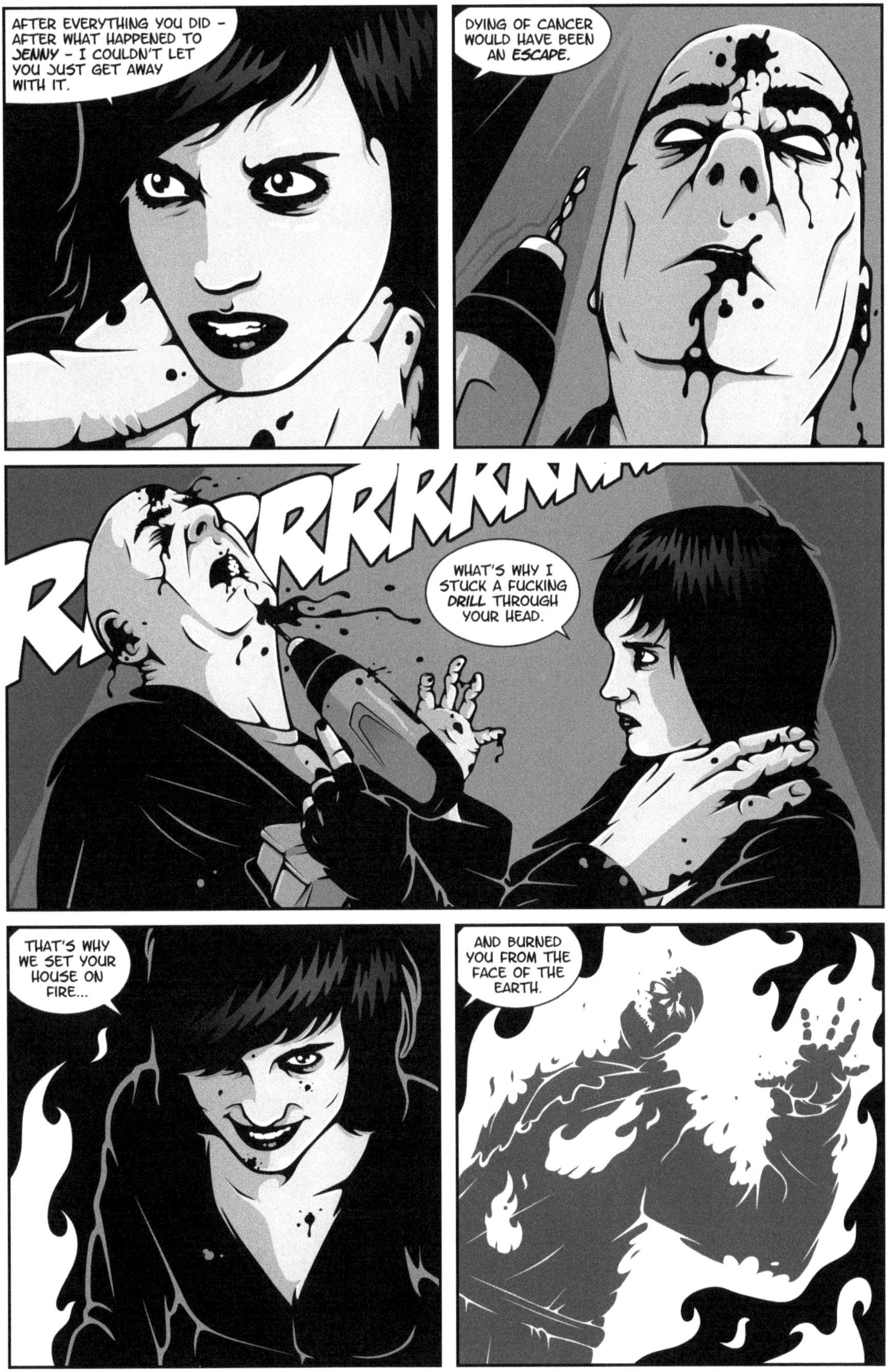
AFTER EVERYTHING YOU DID - AFTER WHAT HAPPENED TO JENNY - I COULDN'T LET YOU JUST GET AWAY WITH IT.
DYING OF CANCER WOULD HAVE BEEN AN ESCAPE.
RRRRRRKKNN
WHAT'S WHY I STUCK A FUCKING DRILL THROUGH YOUR HEAD.
THAT'S WHY WE SET YOUR HOUSE ON FIRE...
AND BURNED YOU FROM THE FACE OF THE EARTH.

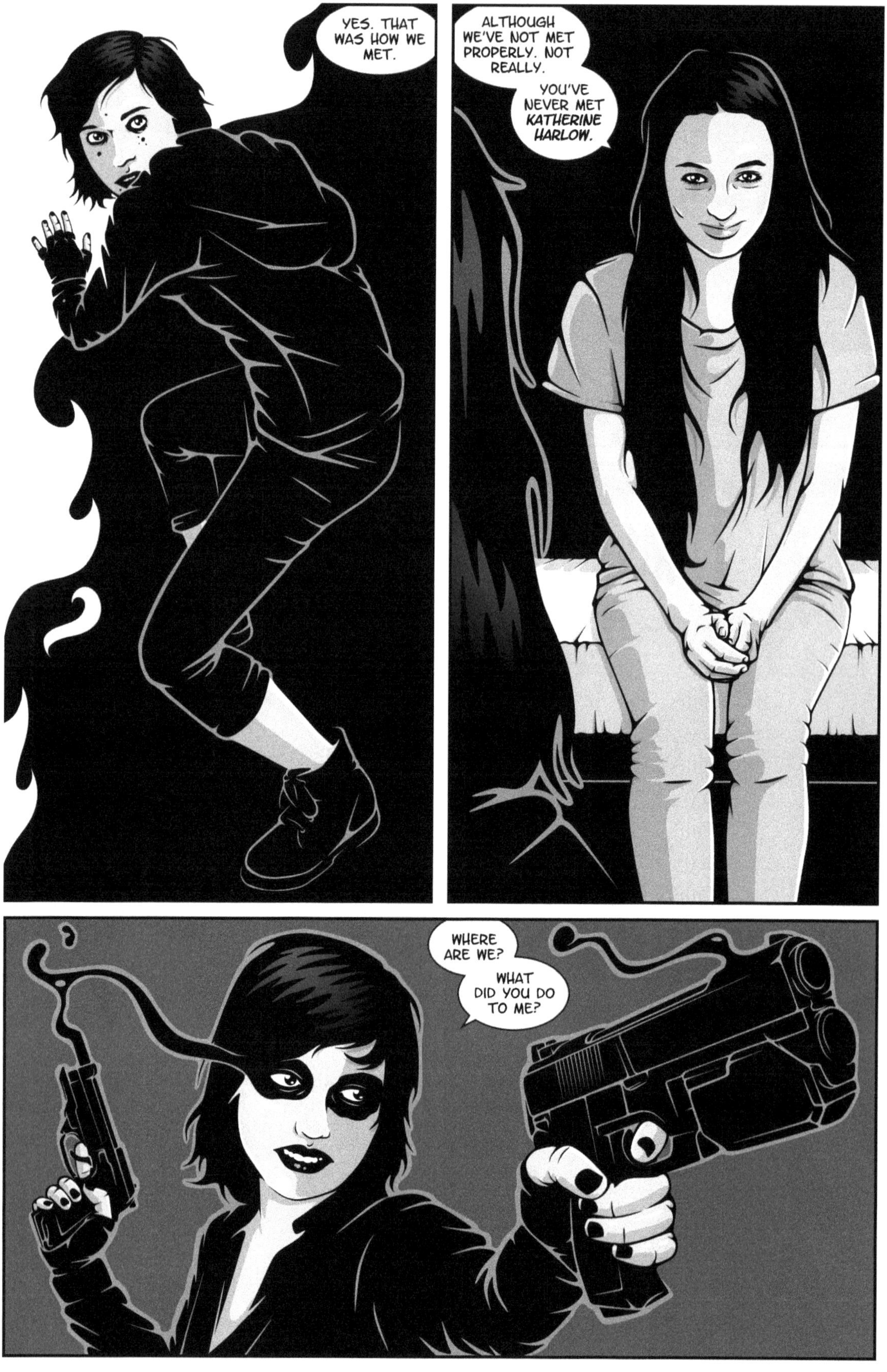
YES. THAT WAS HOW WE MET.
ALTHOUGH WE'VE NOT MET PROPERLY. NOT REALLY.
YOU'VE NEVER MET *KATHERINE HARLOW.*
WHERE ARE WE?
WHAT DID YOU DO TO ME?

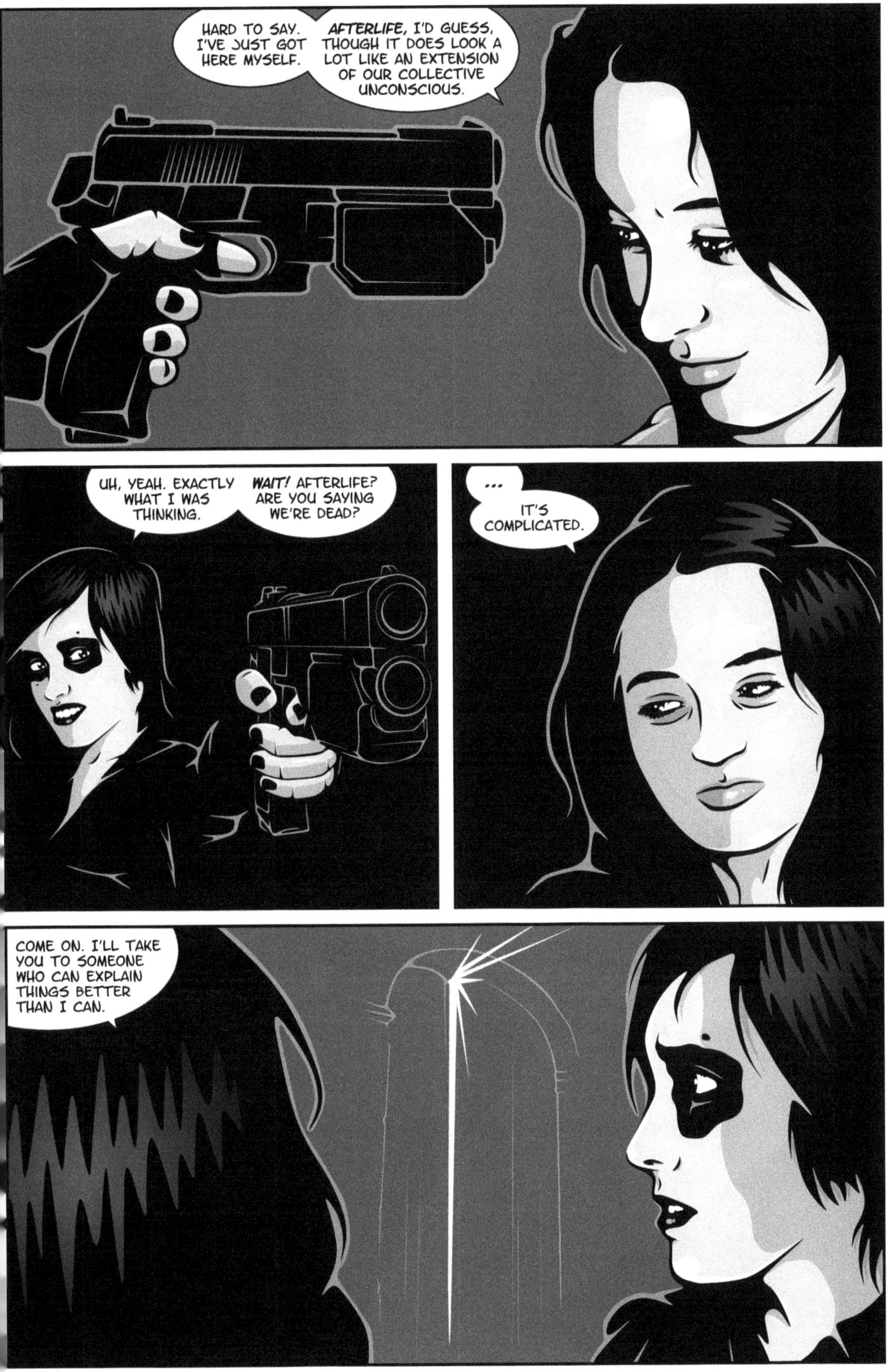
HARD TO SAY. I'VE JUST GOT HERE MYSELF.
AFTERLIFE, I'D GUESS, THOUGH IT DOES LOOK A LOT LIKE AN EXTENSION OF OUR COLLECTIVE UNCONSCIOUS.
UH, YEAH. EXACTLY WHAT I WAS THINKING.
WAIT! AFTERLIFE? ARE YOU SAYING WE'RE DEAD?
...
IT'S COMPLICATED.
COME ON. I'LL TAKE YOU TO SOMEONE WHO CAN EXPLAIN THINGS BETTER THAN I CAN.

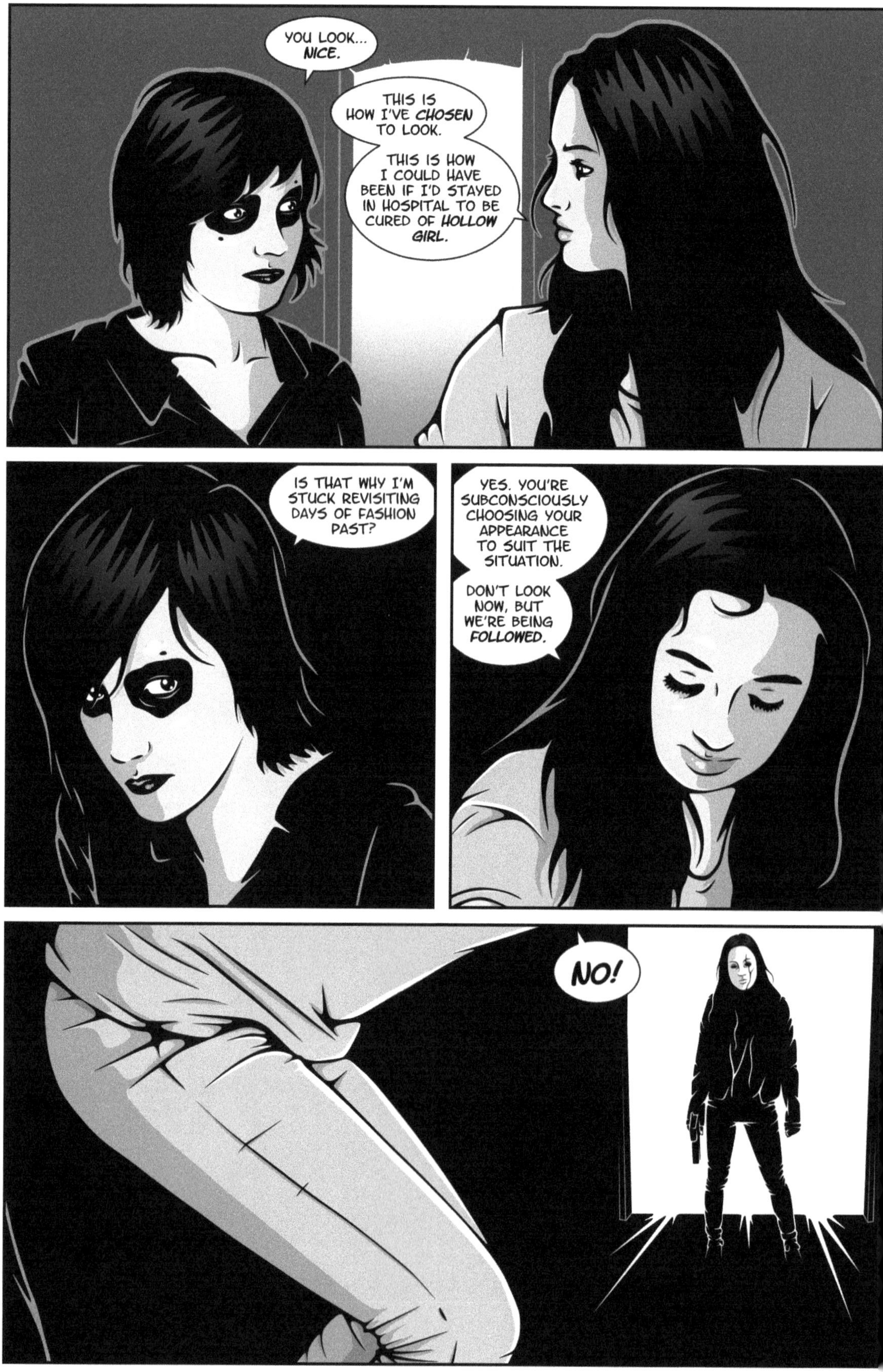
YOU LOOK... NICE.
THIS IS HOW I'VE CHOSEN TO LOOK.
THIS IS HOW I COULD HAVE BEEN IF I'D STAYED IN HOSPITAL TO BE CURED OF HOLLOW GIRL.
IS THAT WHY I'M STUCK REVISITING DAYS OF FASHION PAST?
YES. YOU'RE SUBCONSCIOUSLY CHOOSING YOUR APPEARANCE TO SUIT THE SITUATION.
DON'T LOOK NOW, BUT WE'RE BEING FOLLOWED.
NO!

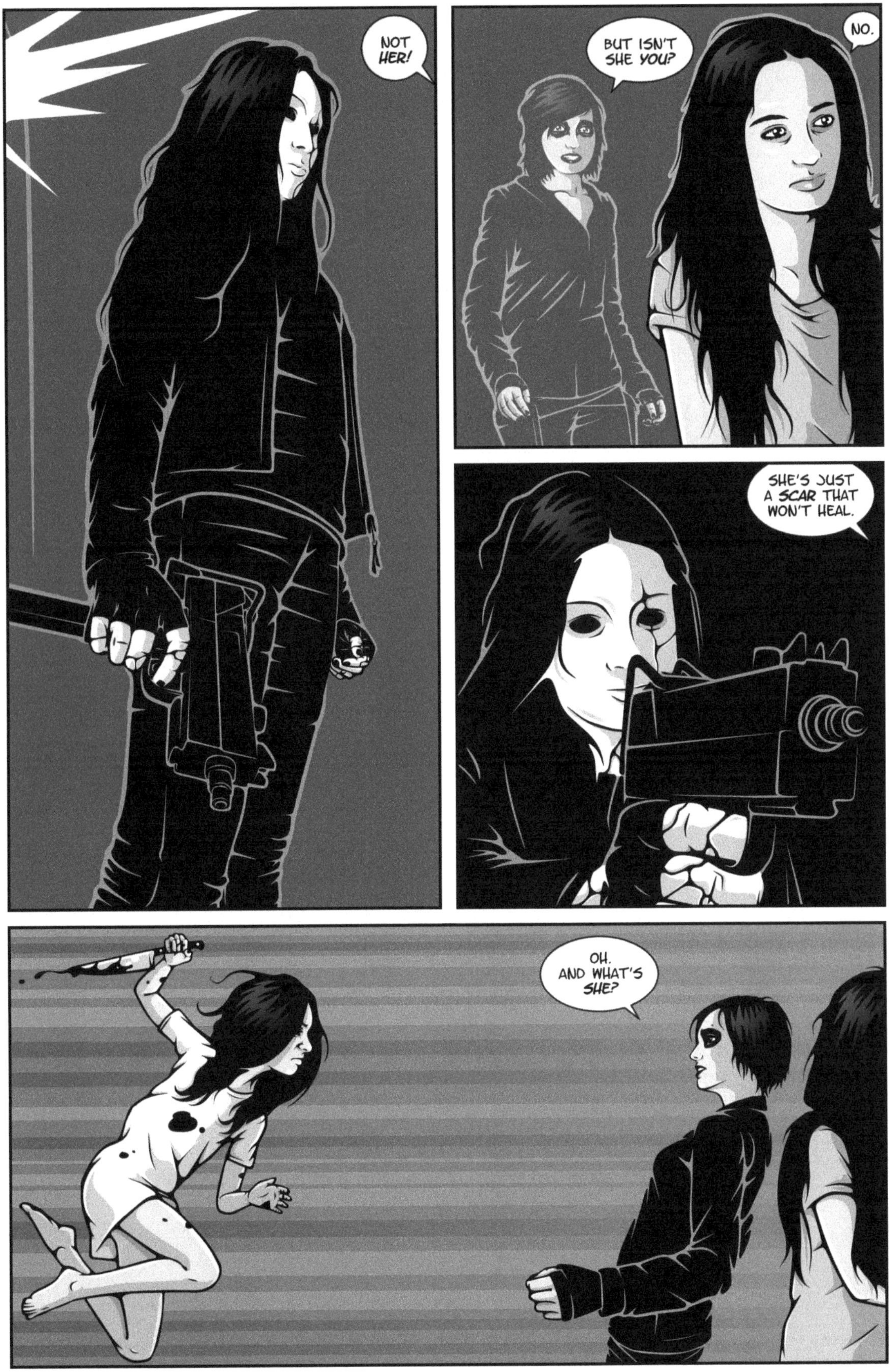
NOT HER!
BUT ISN'T SHE YOU?
NO.
SHE'S JUST A SCAR THAT WON'T HEAL.
OH. AND WHAT'S SHE?

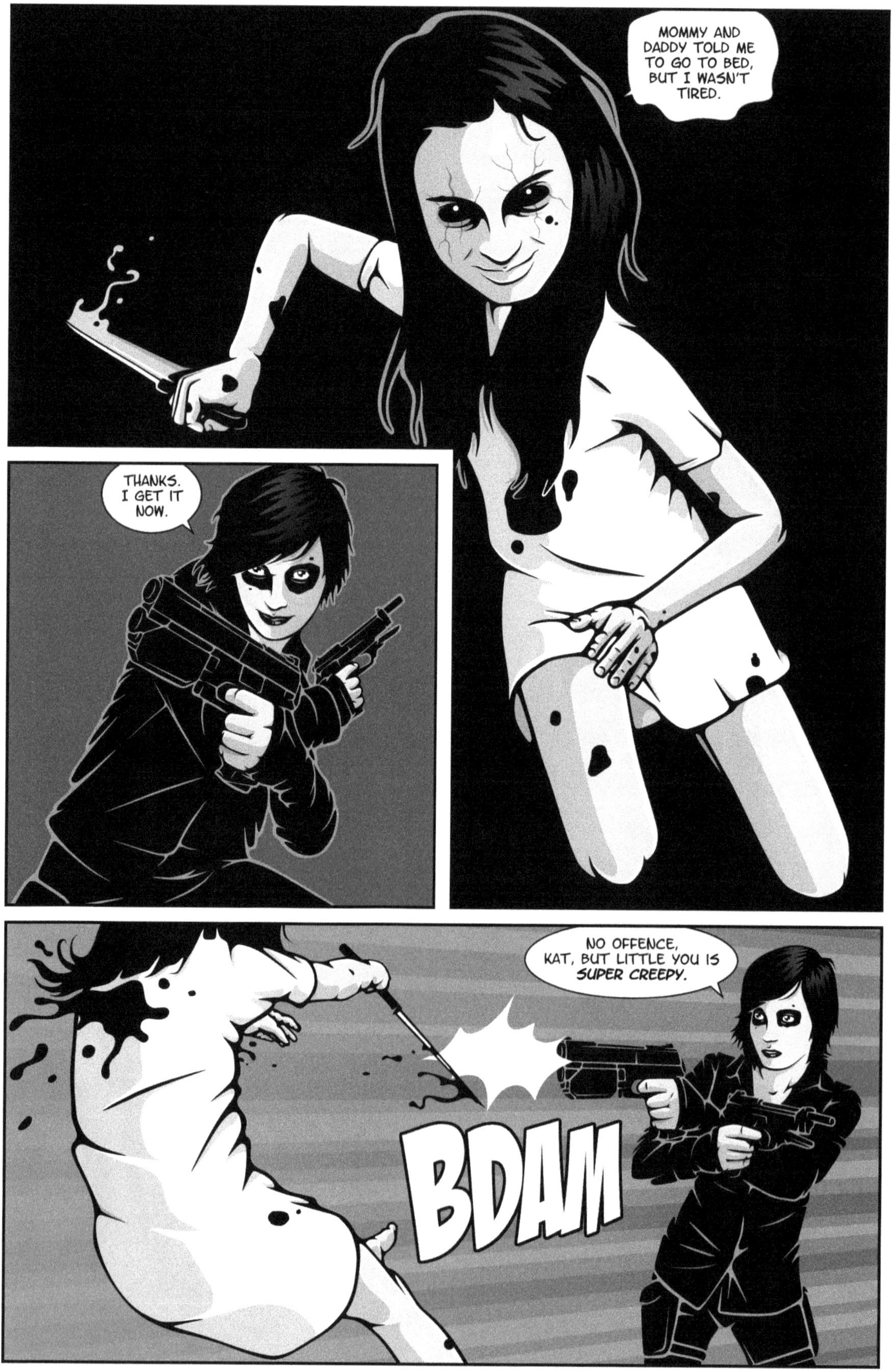
MOMMY AND DADDY TOLD ME TO GO TO BED, BUT I WASN'T TIRED.
THANKS. I GET IT NOW.
NO OFFENCE, KAT, BUT LITTLE YOU IS *SUPER CREEPY.*
BDAM

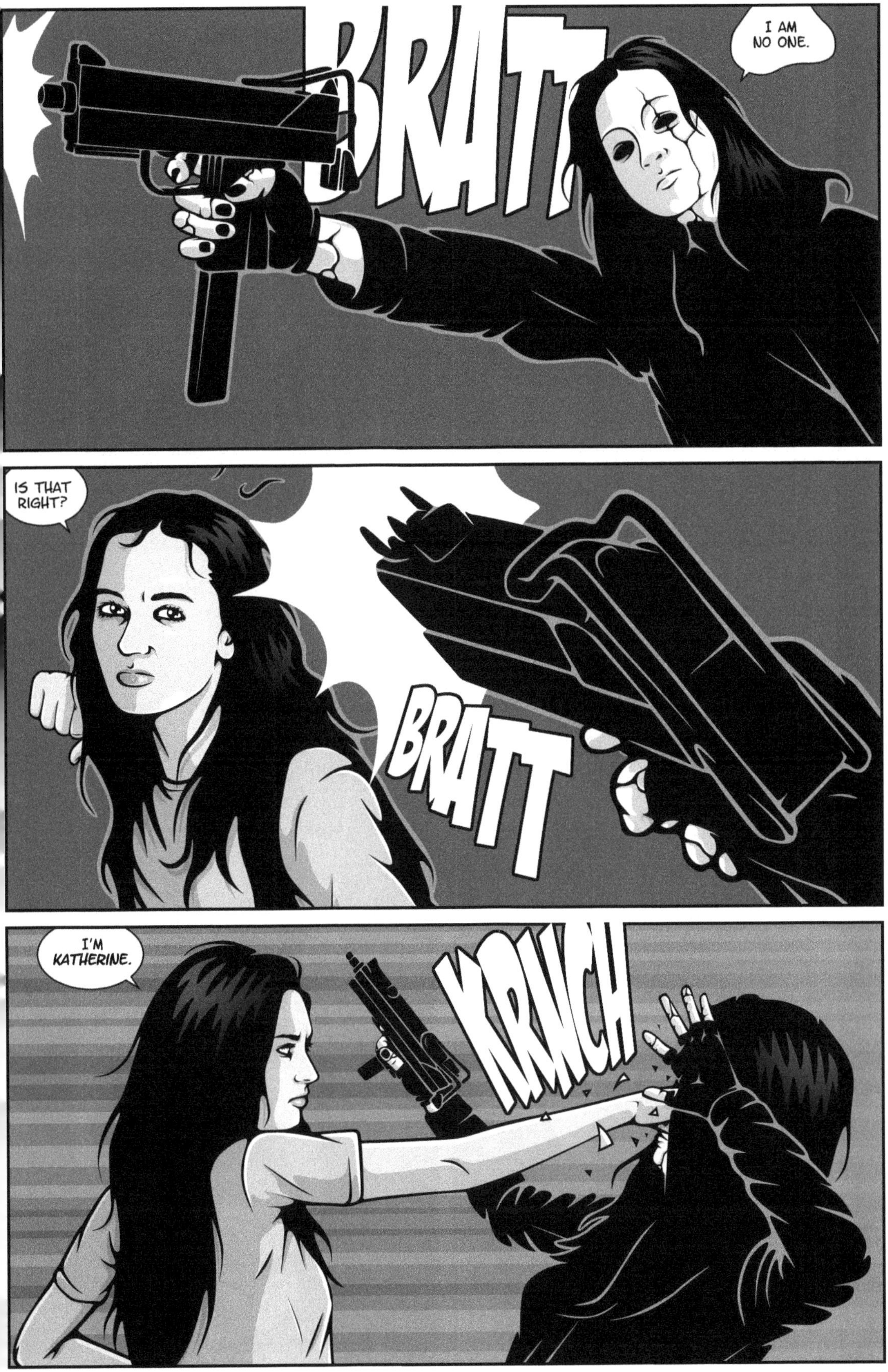
BRATT
I AM NO ONE.
IS THAT RIGHT?
BRATT
I'M KATHERINE.
KRNCH

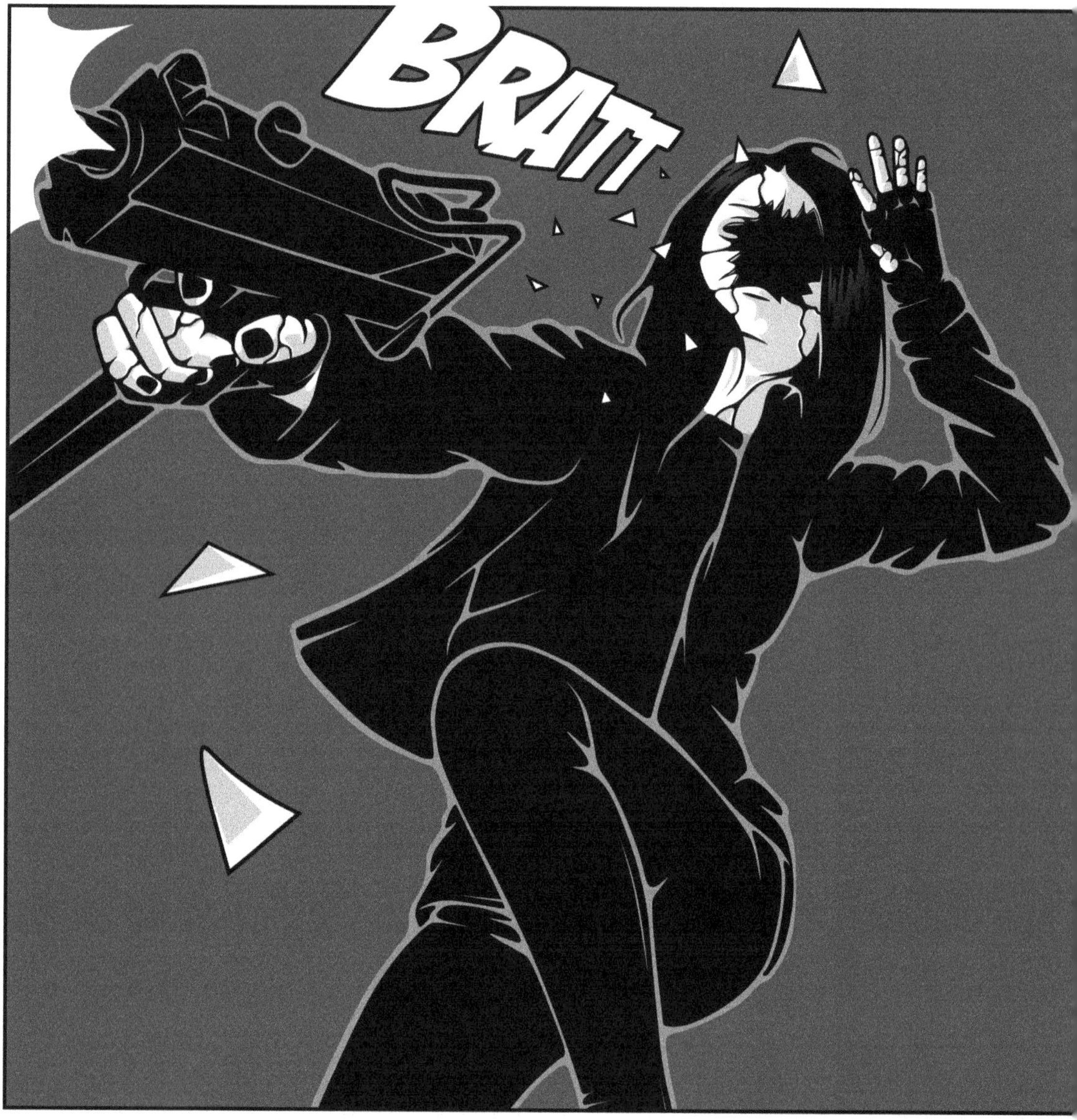
BRATT
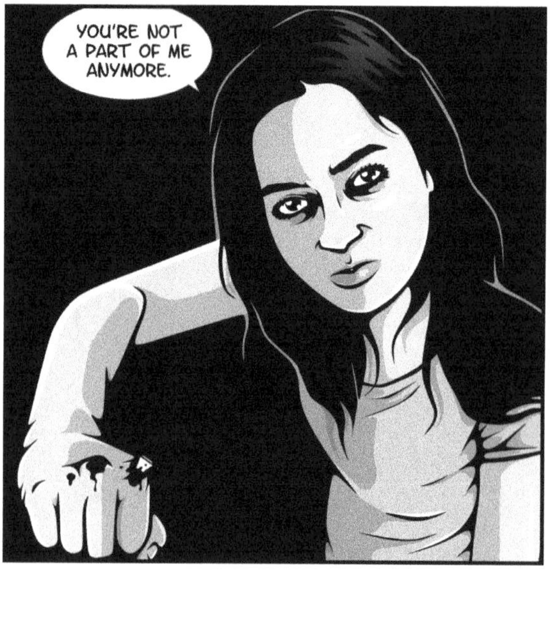
YOU'RE NOT A PART OF ME ANYMORE.
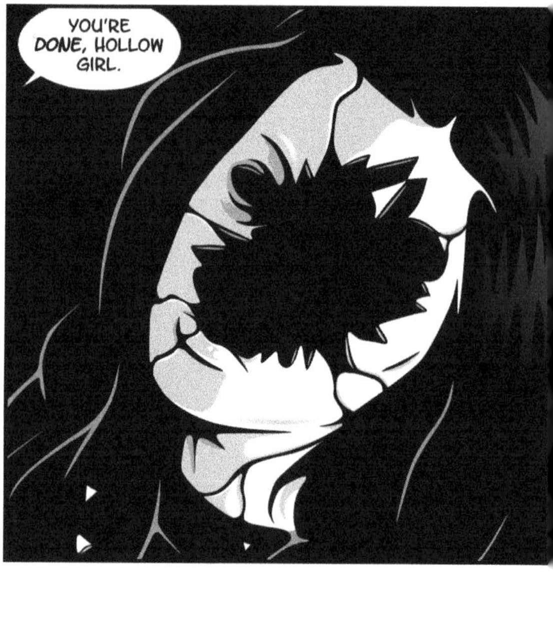
YOU'RE DONE, HOLLOW GIRL.

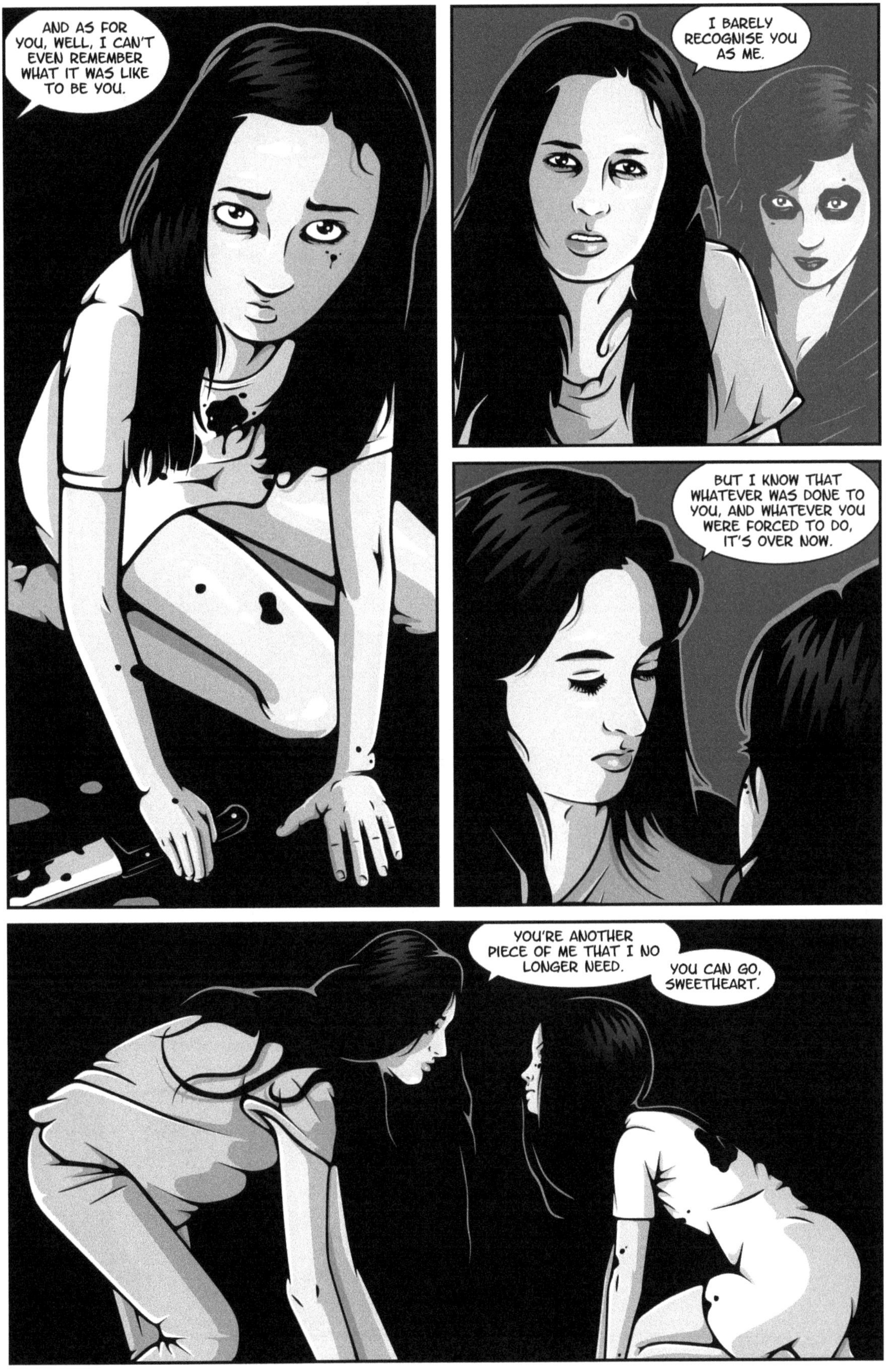
AND AS FOR YOU, WELL, I CAN'T EVEN REMEMBER WHAT IT WAS LIKE TO BE YOU.
I BARELY RECOGNISE YOU AS ME.
BUT I KNOW THAT WHATEVER WAS DONE TO YOU, AND WHATEVER YOU WERE FORCED TO DO, IT'S OVER NOW.
YOU'RE ANOTHER PIECE OF ME THAT I NO LONGER NEED.
YOU CAN GO, SWEETHEART.

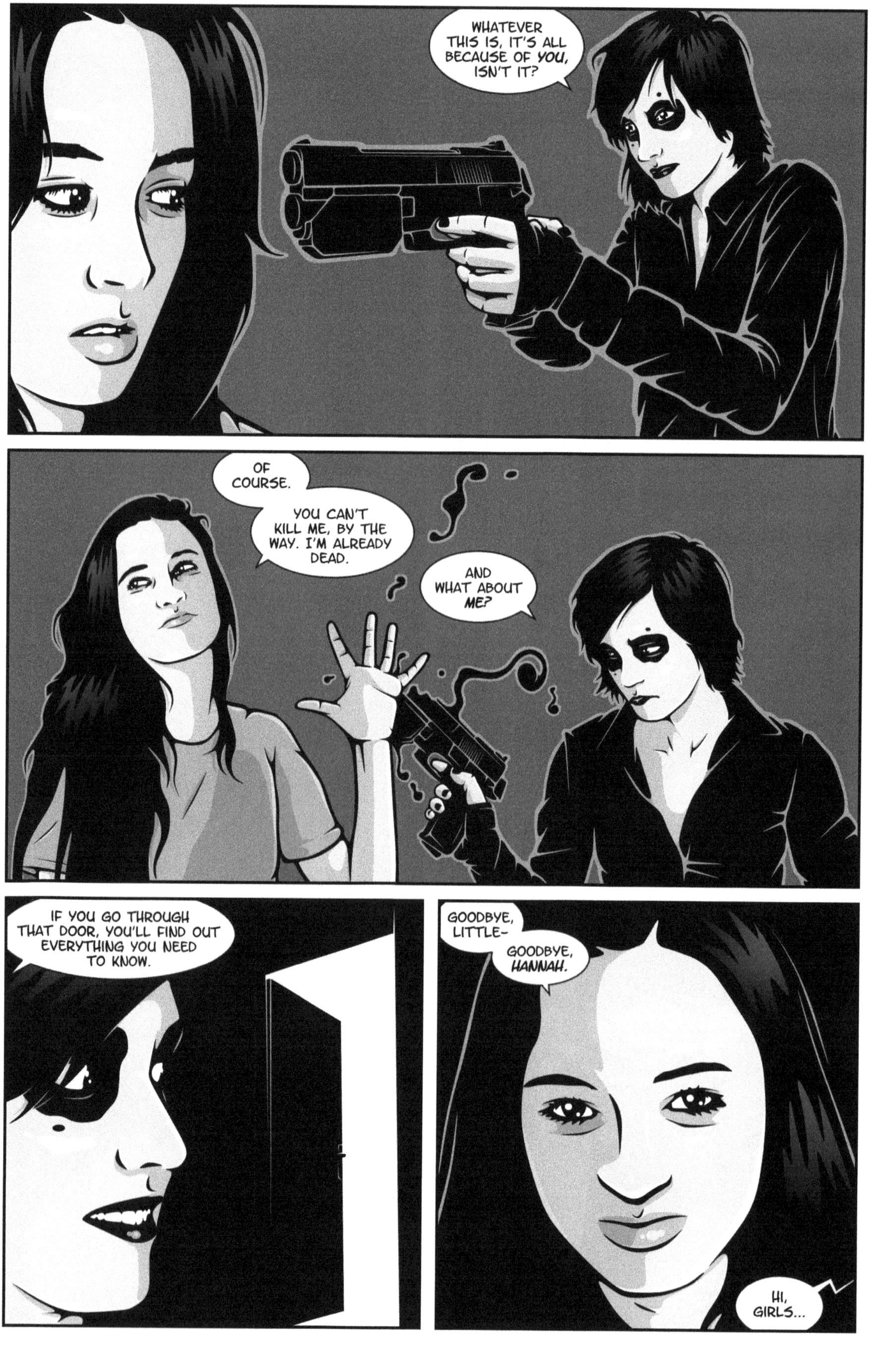
WHATEVER THIS IS, IT'S ALL BECAUSE OF YOU, ISN'T IT?
OF COURSE.
YOU CAN'T KILL ME, BY THE WAY. I'M ALREADY DEAD.
AND WHAT ABOUT ME?
IF YOU GO THROUGH THAT DOOR, YOU'LL FIND OUT EVERYTHING YOU NEED TO KNOW.
GOODBYE, LITTLE-
GOODBYE, HANNAH.
HI, GIRLS...

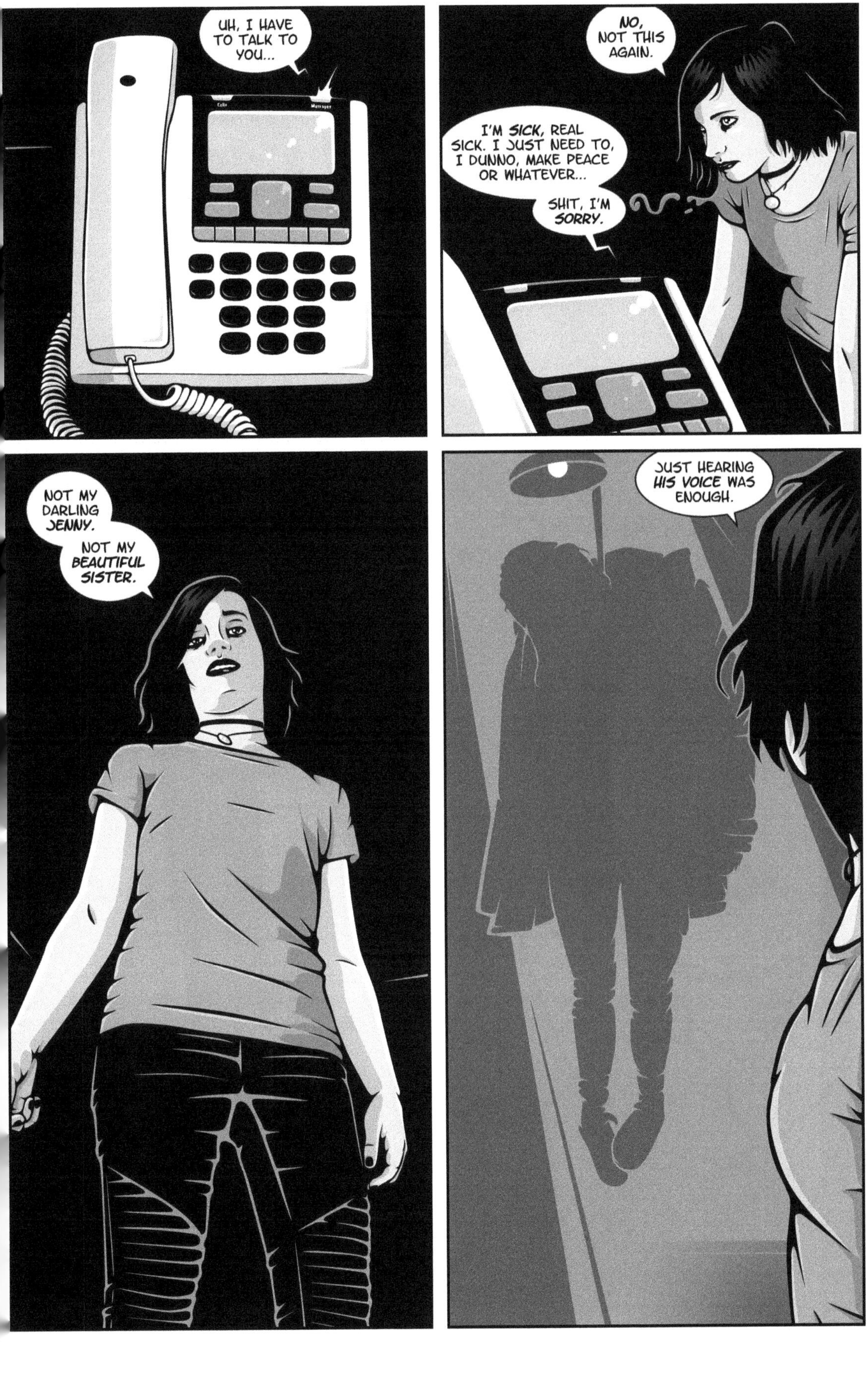

UH, I HAVE TO TALK TO YOU...
NO, NOT THIS AGAIN.
I'M SICK, REAL SICK. I JUST NEED TO, I DUNNO, MAKE PEACE OR WHATEVER...
SHIT, I'M SORRY.
NOT MY DARLING JENNY.
NOT MY BEAUTIFUL SISTER.
JUST HEARING HIS VOICE WAS ENOUGH.

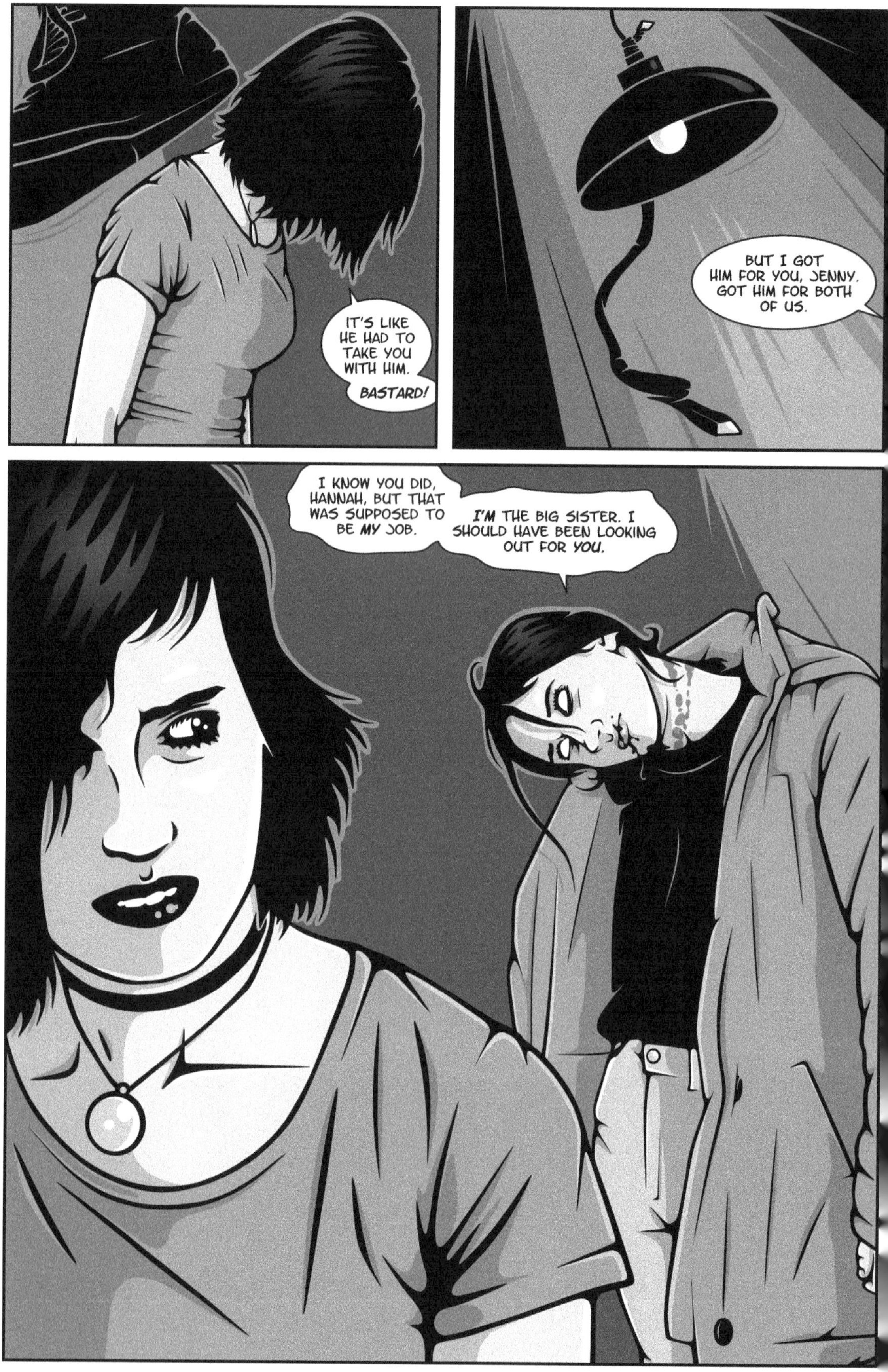
IT'S LIKE HE HAD TO TAKE YOU WITH HIM.
BASTARD!
BUT I GOT HIM FOR YOU, JENNY. GOT HIM FOR BOTH OF US.
I KNOW YOU DID, HANNAH, BUT THAT WAS SUPPOSED TO BE MY JOB.
I'M THE BIG SISTER. I SHOULD HAVE BEEN LOOKING OUT FOR YOU.

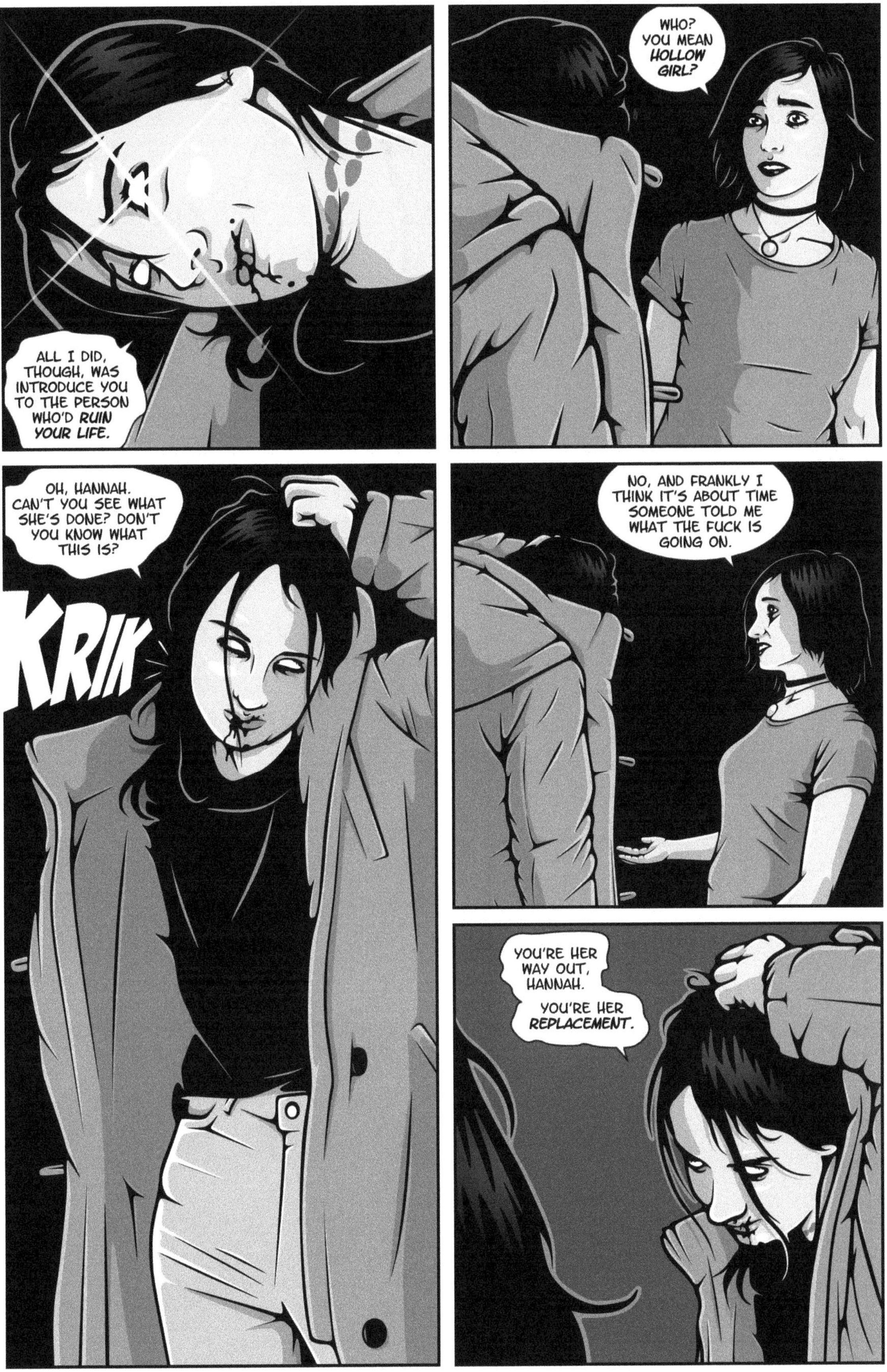
ALL I DID, THOUGH, WAS INTRODUCE YOU TO THE PERSON WHO'D RUIN YOUR LIFE.
WHO? YOU MEAN HOLLOW GIRL?
OH, HANNAH. CAN'T YOU SEE WHAT SHE'S DONE? DON'T YOU KNOW WHAT THIS IS?
KRIK
NO, AND FRANKLY I THINK IT'S ABOUT TIME SOMEONE TOLD ME WHAT THE FUCK IS GOING ON.
YOU'RE HER WAY OUT, HANNAH.
YOU'RE HER REPLACEMENT.

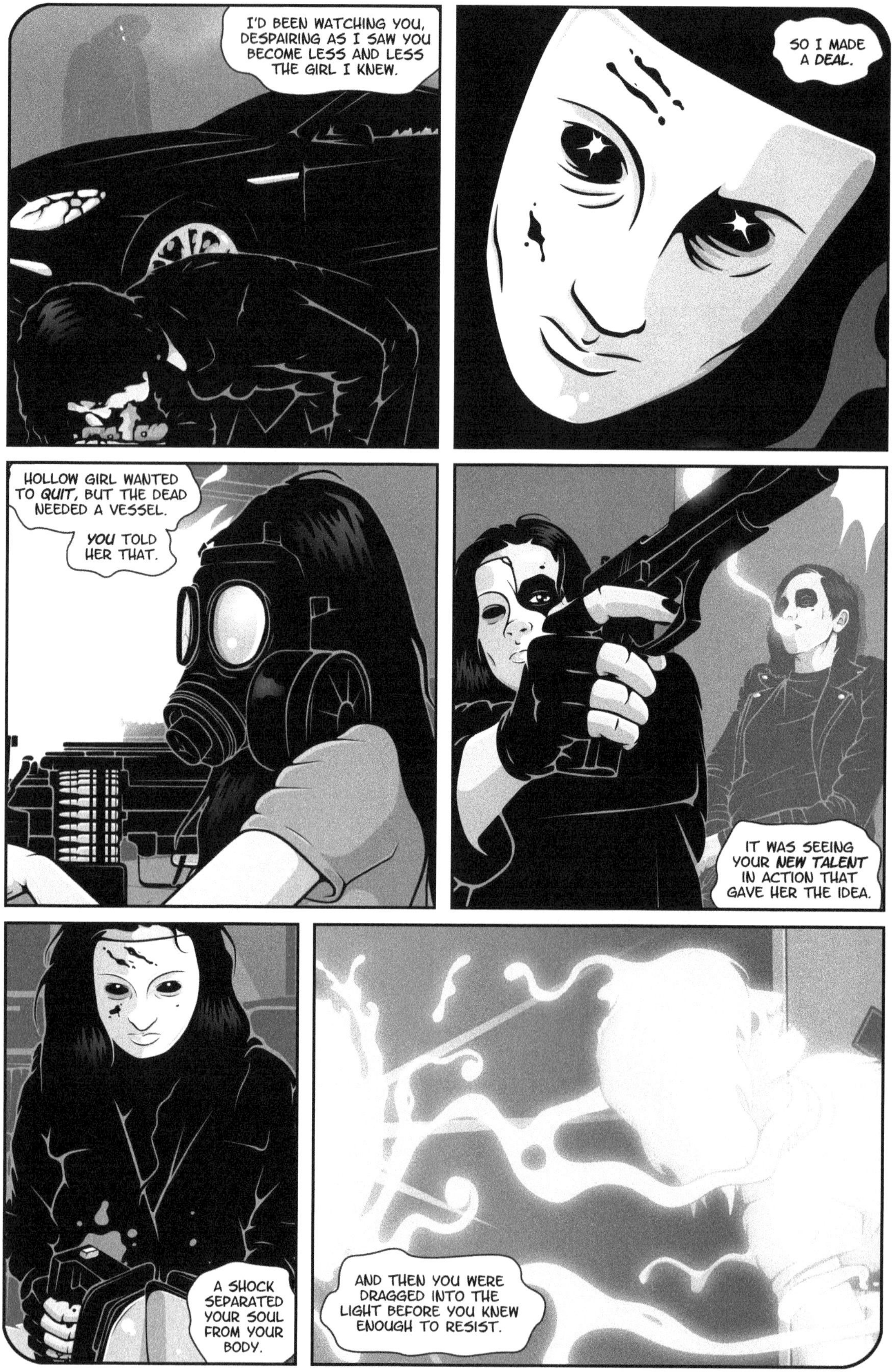
I'D BEEN WATCHING YOU, DESPAIRING AS I SAW YOU BECOME LESS AND LESS THE GIRL I KNEW.
SO I MADE A *DEAL.*
HOLLOW GIRL WANTED TO *QUIT*, BUT THE DEAD NEEDED A VESSEL.
YOU TOLD HER THAT.
IT WAS SEEING YOUR *NEW TALENT* IN ACTION THAT GAVE HER THE IDEA.
A SHOCK SEPARATED YOUR SOUL FROM YOUR BODY.
AND THEN YOU WERE DRAGGED INTO THE LIGHT BEFORE YOU KNEW ENOUGH TO RESIST.

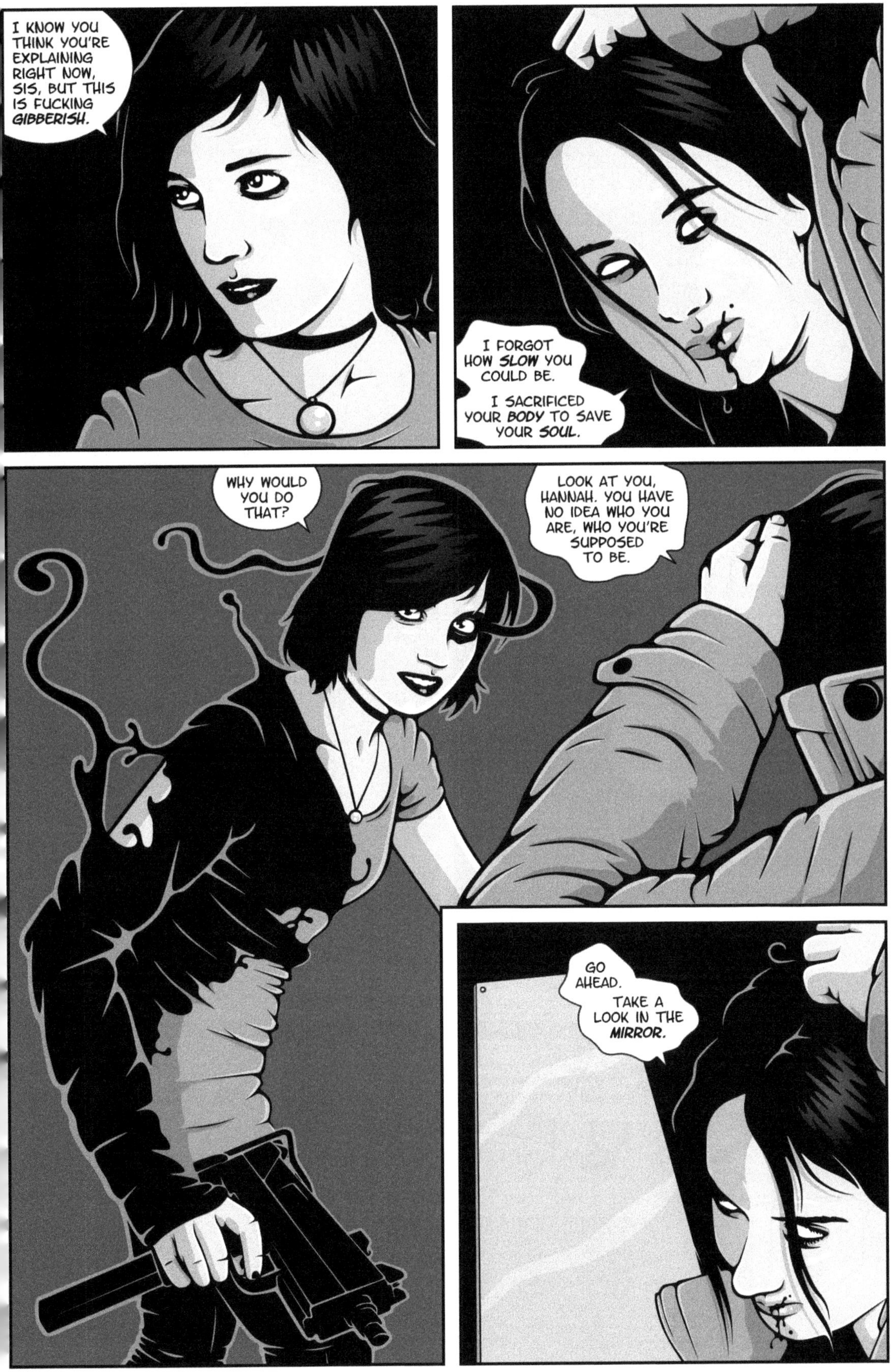
I KNOW YOU THINK YOU'RE EXPLAINING RIGHT NOW, SIS, BUT THIS IS FUCKING GIBBERISH.
I FORGOT HOW SLOW YOU COULD BE.
I SACRIFICED YOUR BODY TO SAVE YOUR SOUL.
WHY WOULD YOU DO THAT?
LOOK AT YOU, HANNAH. YOU HAVE NO IDEA WHO YOU ARE, WHO YOU'RE SUPPOSED TO BE.
GO AHEAD.
TAKE A LOOK IN THE MIRROR.

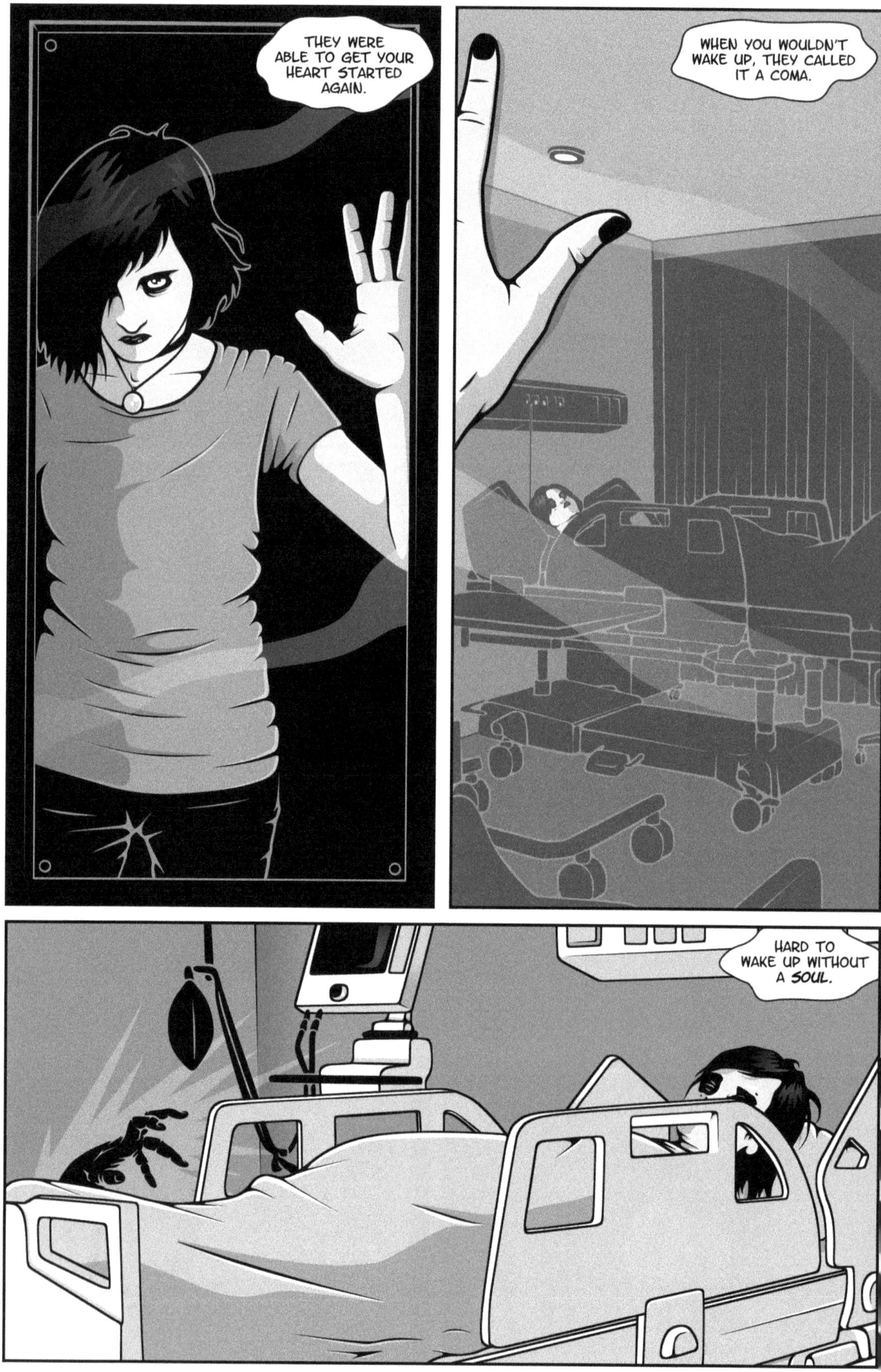
THEY WERE ABLE TO GET YOUR HEART STARTED AGAIN.
WHEN YOU WOULDN'T WAKE UP, THEY CALLED IT A COMA.
HARD TO WAKE UP WITHOUT A **SOUL**.

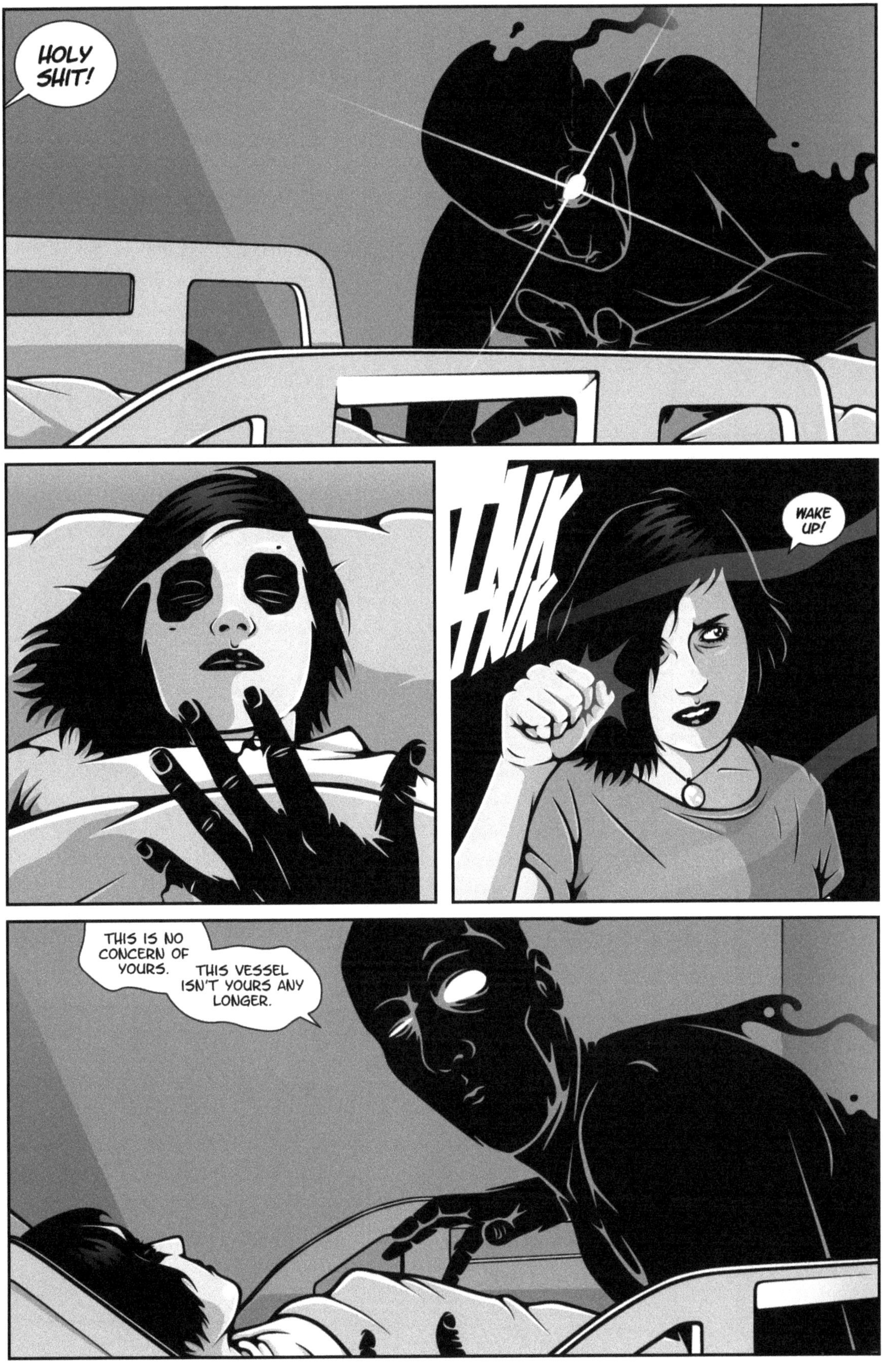
HOLY SHIT!
WAKE UP!
THIS IS NO CONCERN OF YOURS.
THIS VESSEL ISN'T YOURS ANY LONGER.

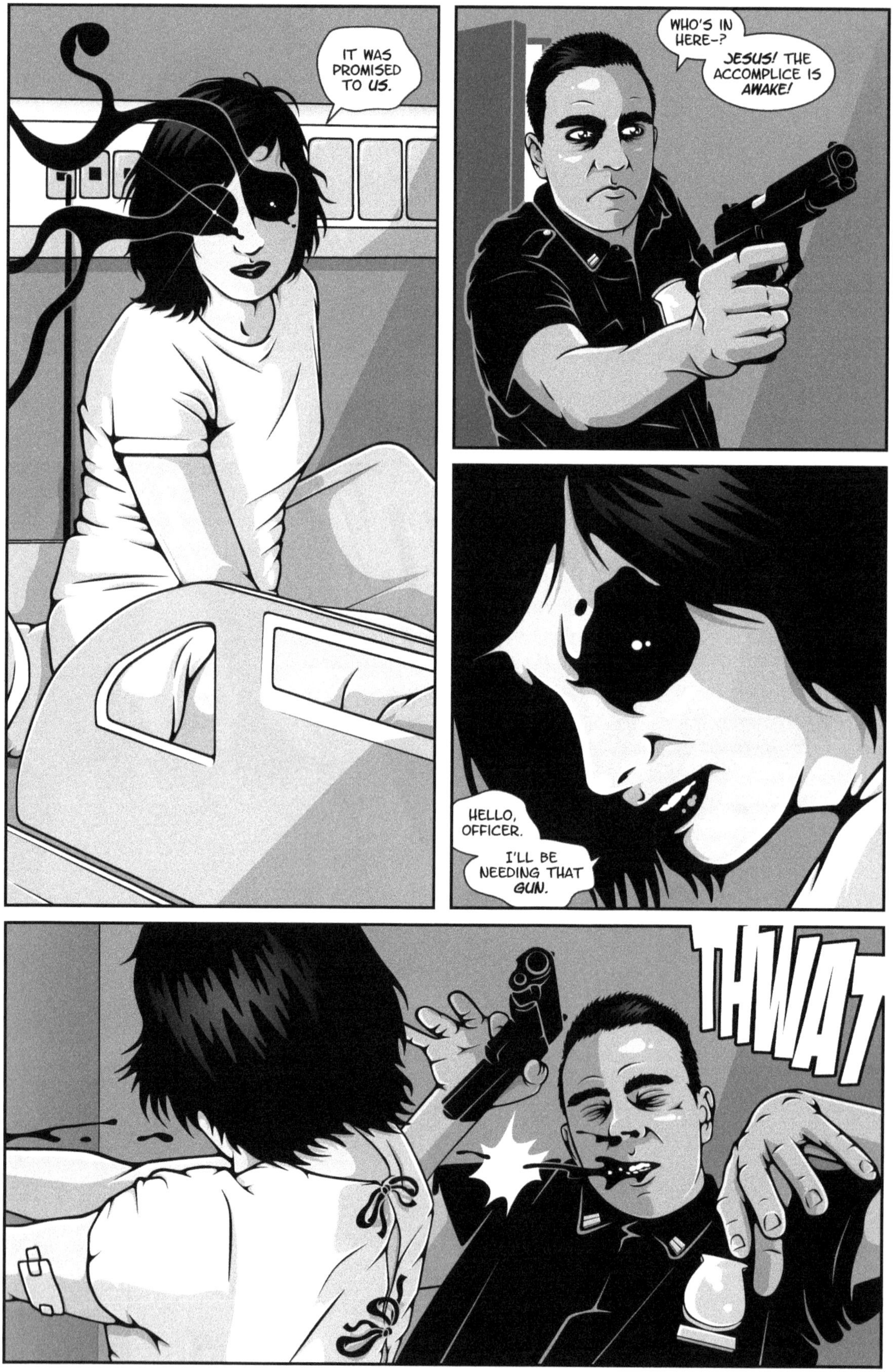
IT WAS PROMISED TO US.
WHO'S IN HERE-?
JESUS! THE ACCOMPLICE IS AWAKE!
HELLO, OFFICER.
I'LL BE NEEDING THAT GUN.
THWAT

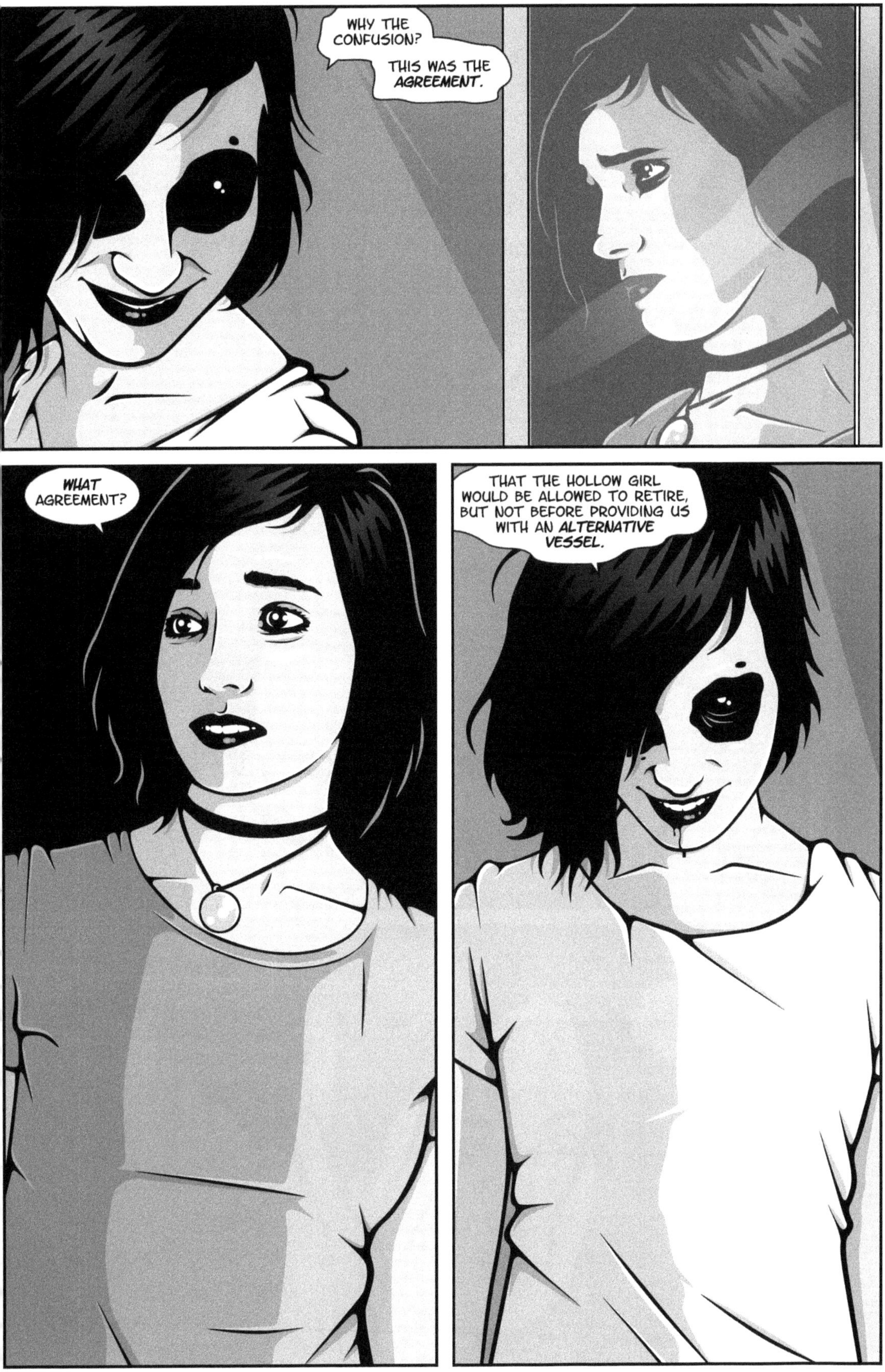
WHY THE CONFUSION?
THIS WAS THE AGREEMENT.
WHAT AGREEMENT?
THAT THE HOLLOW GIRL WOULD BE ALLOWED TO RETIRE, BUT NOT BEFORE PROVIDING US WITH AN ALTERNATIVE VESSEL.

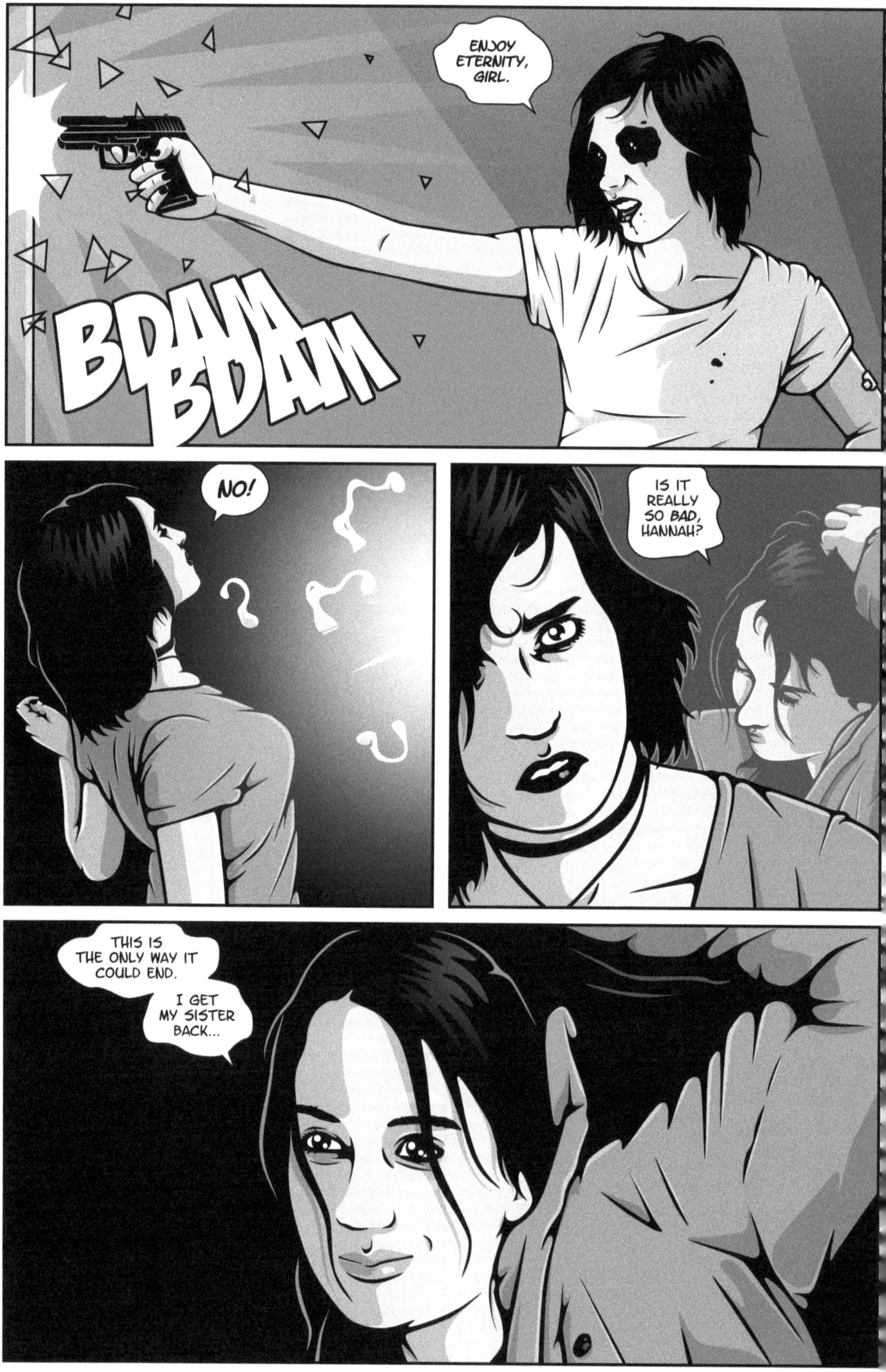
ENJOY ETERNITY, GIRL.
BDAM
BDAM
NO!
IS IT REALLY SO BAD, HANNAH?
THIS IS THE ONLY WAY IT COULD END.
I GET MY SISTER BACK...

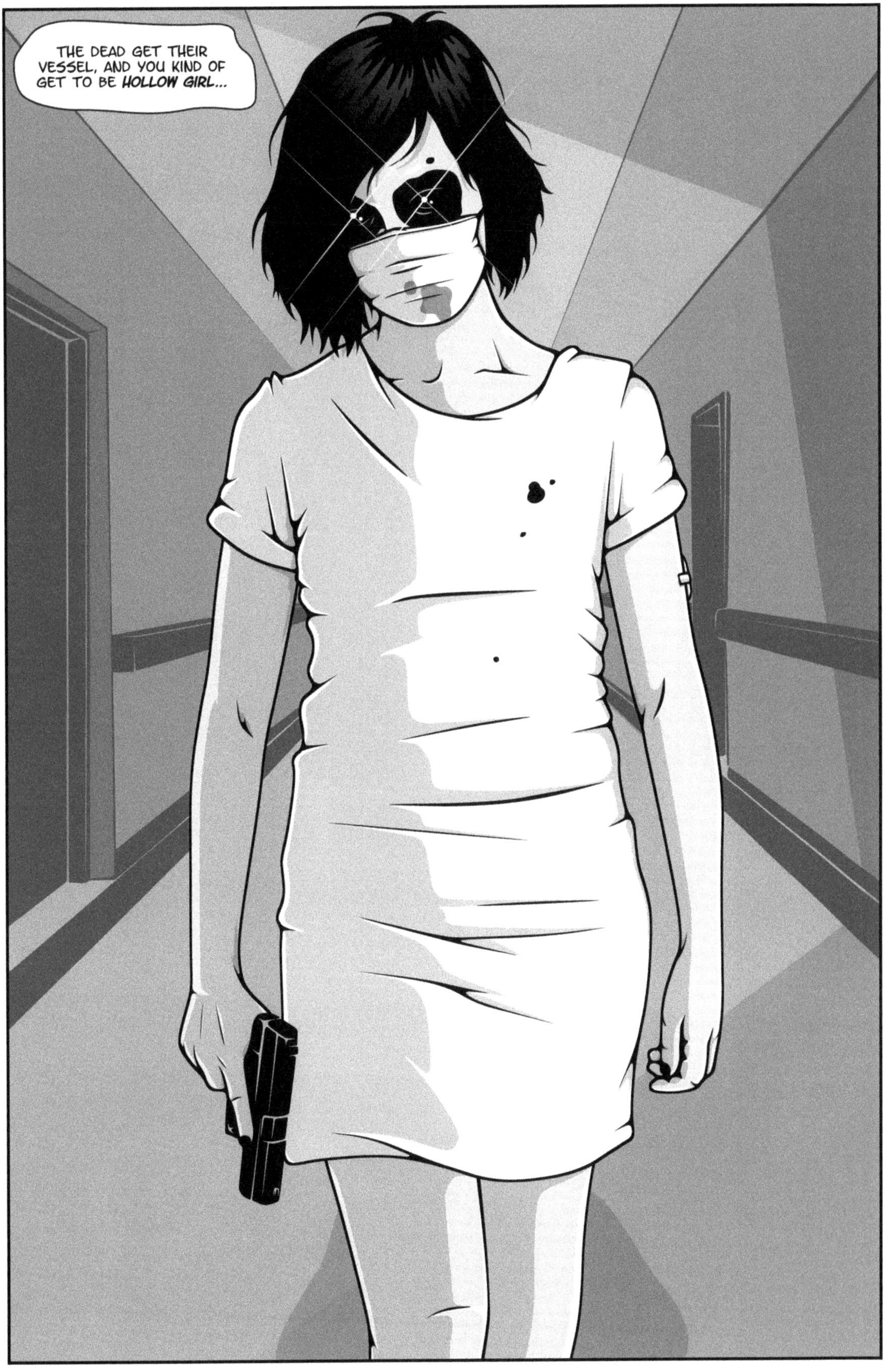
THE DEAD GET THEIR VESSEL, AND YOU KIND OF GET TO BE HOLLOW GIRL...

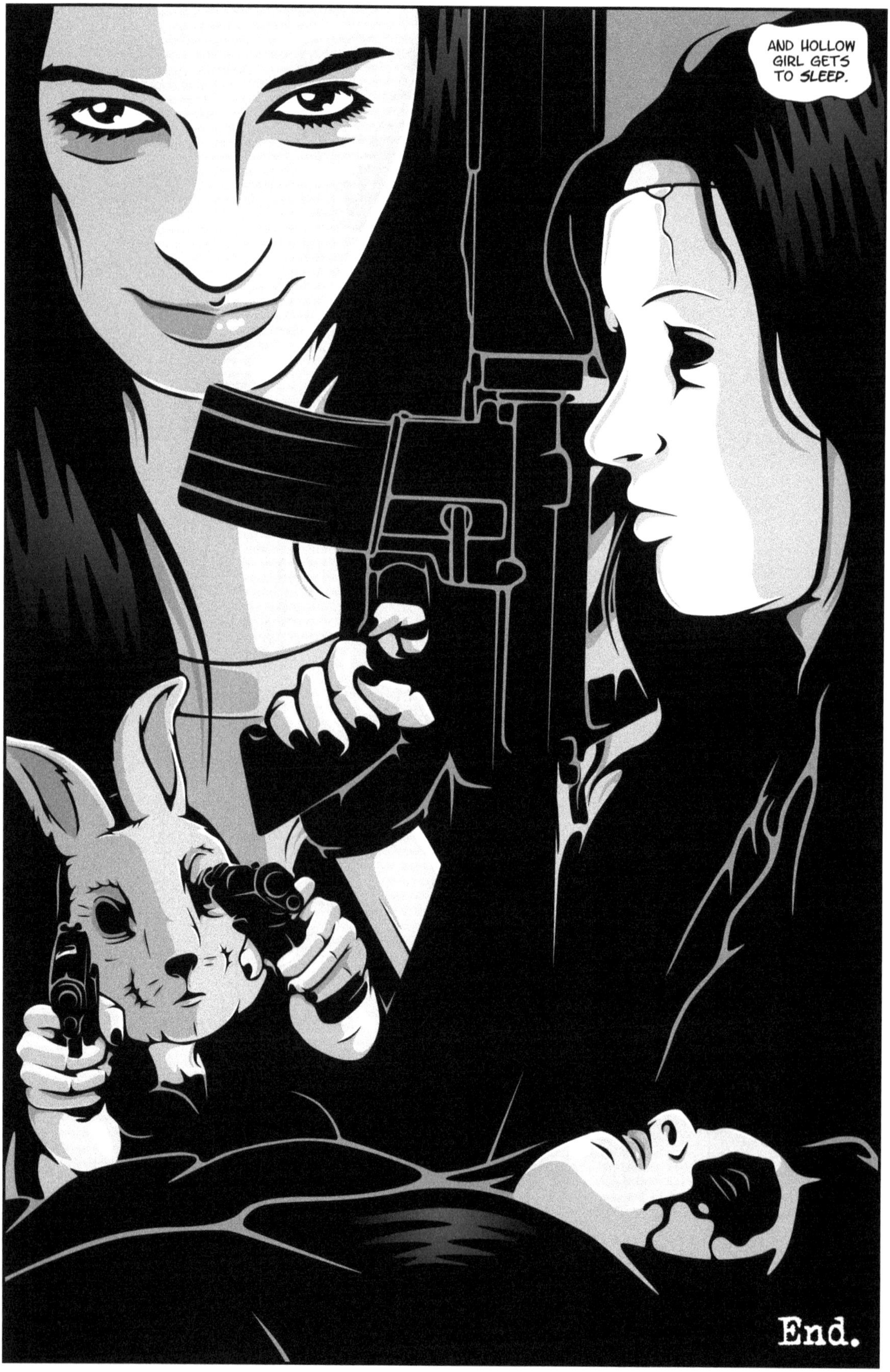
AND HOLLOW GIRL GETS TO SLEEP.
End.

Bonus Content

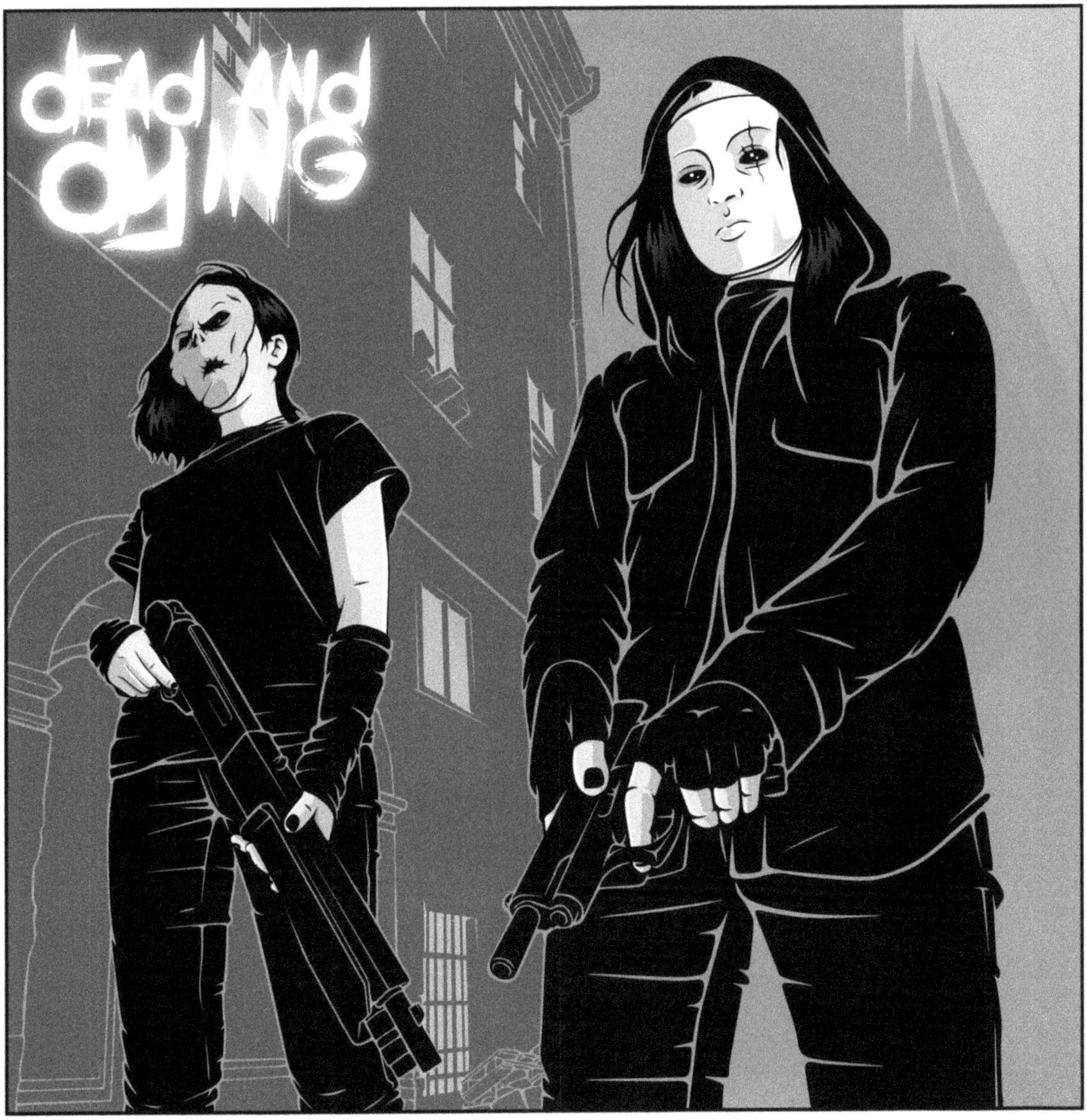
dead and dying

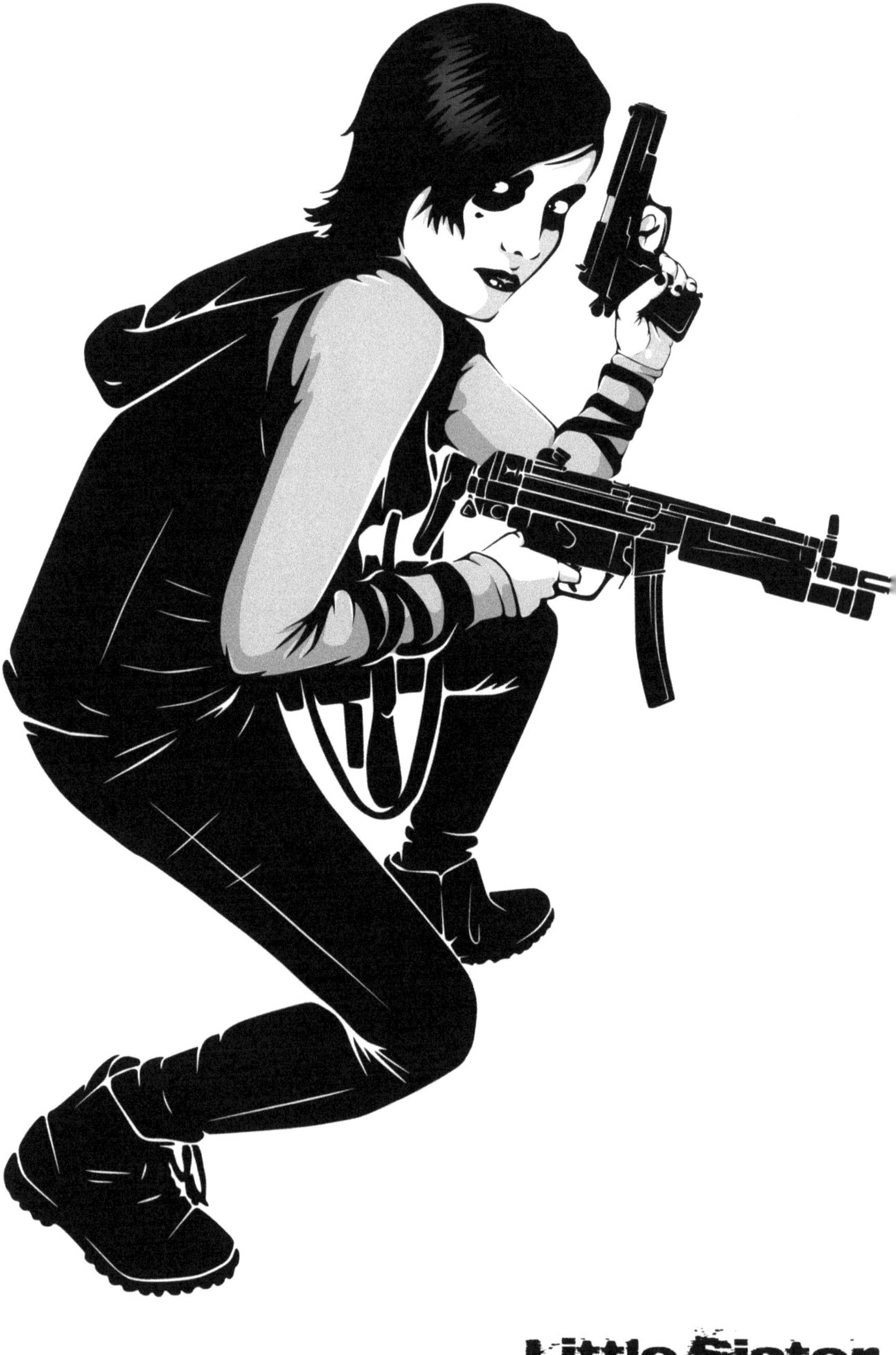

Little Sister
Character Sketch

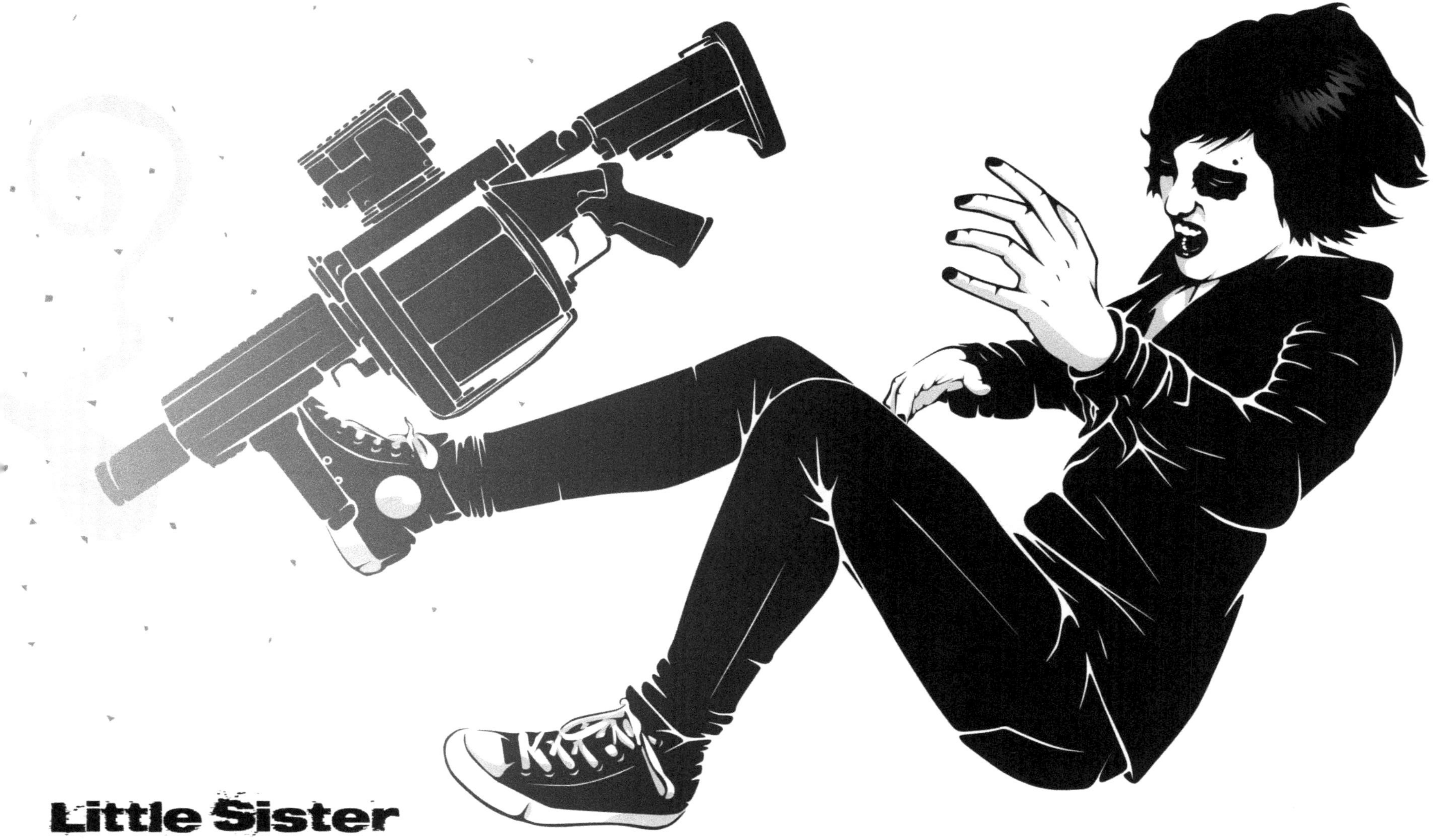

Little Sister
Character Sketch

Cover Art

Original Inks by Stefano Cardoselli

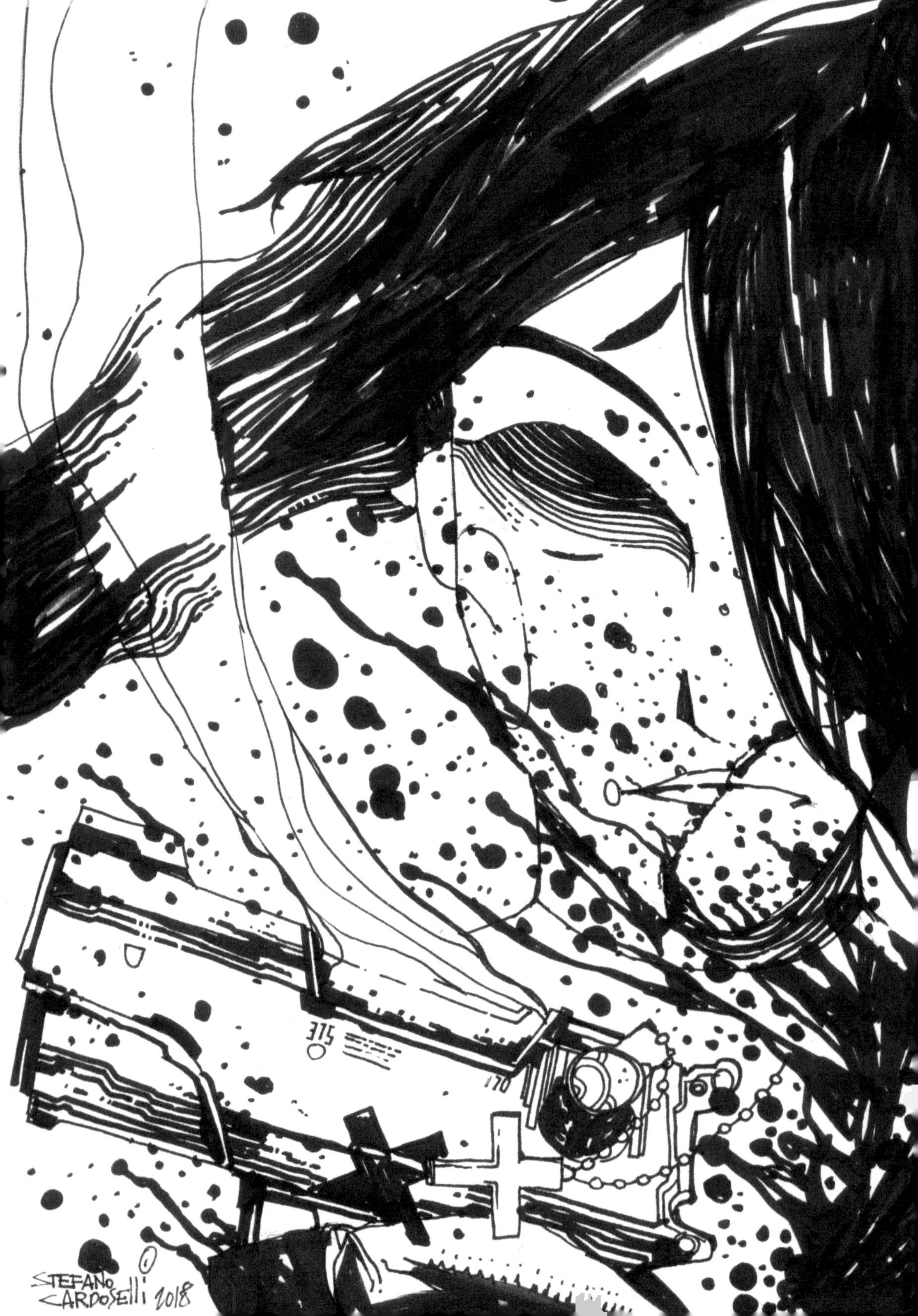
©
STEFANO
CARDOSELLI 2018

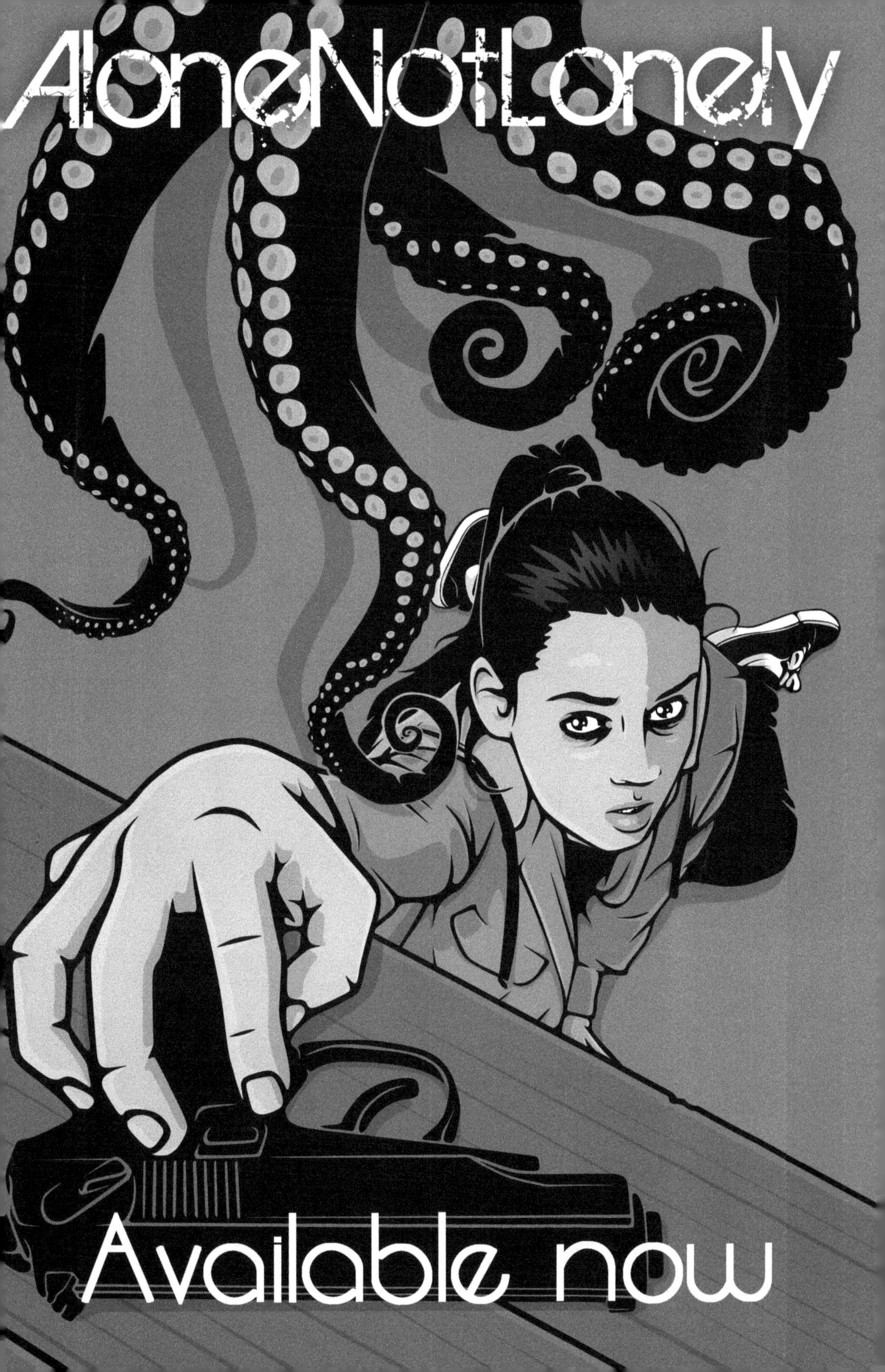
AloneNotLonely
Available now

ABOUT THE AUTHOR

Luke Cooper is the creator of *Hollow Girl*, *AloneNotLonely*, *Figments*, *Pumpernickel* and *A Glimpse of Hell*, and artist on the award winning *GoodCopBadCop*, *Wolf Country* and *Burlap: Death Waits for No One*.

@lmjcooper

Hollow Girl: The Comic Art of Luke Cooper

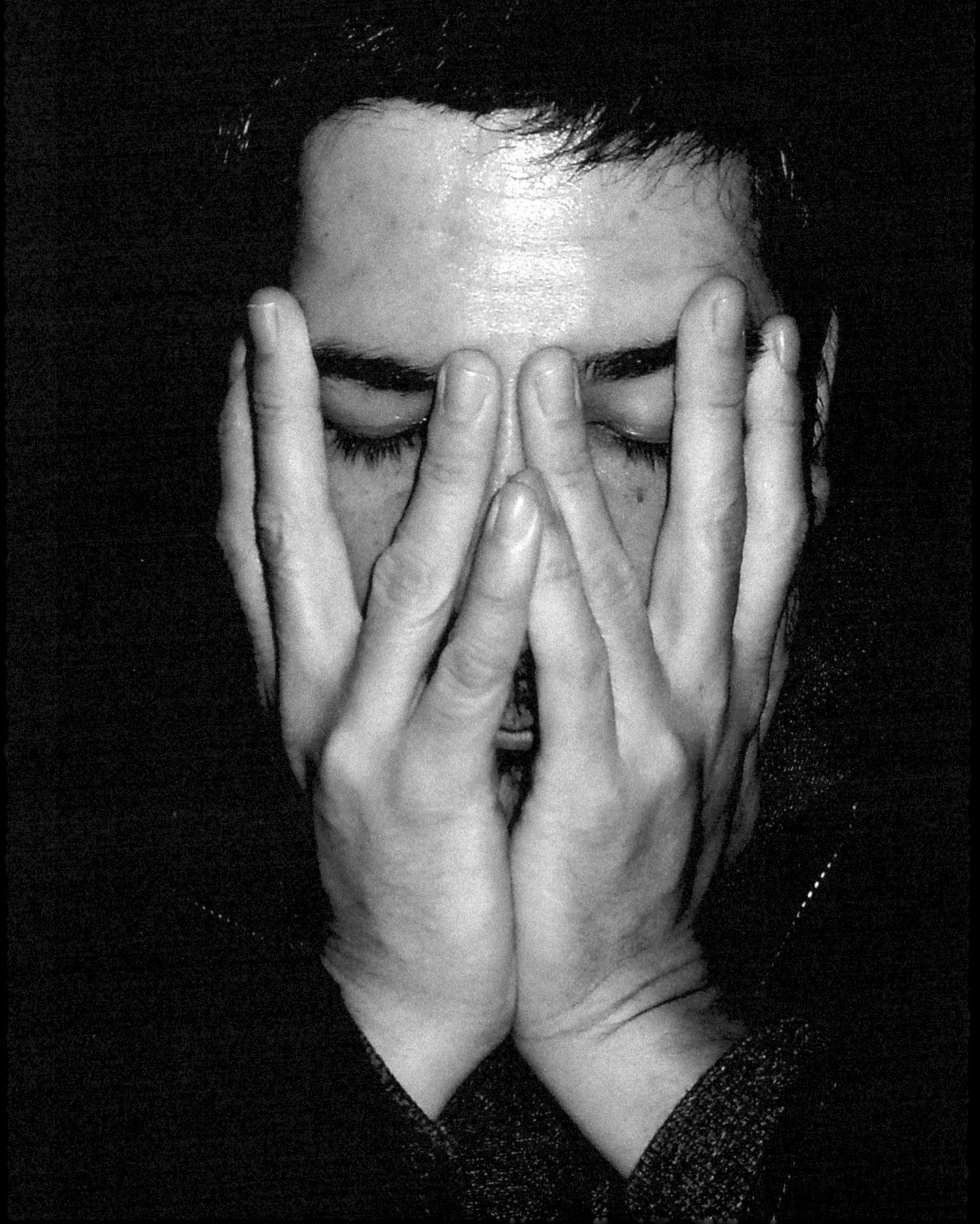

Ingram Content Group UK Ltd.
Milton Keynes UK
UKHW050727020523
421098UK00008B/319